From the Publisher's Desk

Dear readers,

I am thrilled to welcome you to the first edition of our brand-new martial arts magazine. We are proud to present a collection of insightful articles and personal stories from our local martial arts community, highlighting the diverse range of styles and experiences that can be found here in West Australia.

I want to extend a heartfelt thank you to all our contributors who have poured their hearts and souls into their articles. Each piece is a unique and valuable contribution to the martial arts world, and we are honoured to have the opportunity to share them with our readers.

To our subscribers, we are deeply grateful for your support and enthusiasm. Without you, this magazine would not be possible. We are committed to bringing you the best and most engaging content possible, and we hope that this first edition sets the tone for many more to come.

Yours sincerely
Vanessa McKay

All content published in MAWA Magazine, including articles, images, and other media, is the property of the magazine and is protected by copyright law. The author retains the copyright to their individual work, but by submitting their work to MAWA Magazine, they grant the magazine an exclusive, perpetual, and irrevocable license to publish and distribute their work in all formats, including print, digital, and online media. No part of MAWA Magazine may be reproduced, distributed, or transmitted in any form or by any means, including photocopying, recording, or other electronic or mechanical methods, without the prior written permission of the magazine.

MAWA Magazine respects the intellectual property rights of others and expects its contributors and readers to do the same. If you believe that your copyrighted work has been used in a way that constitutes copyright infringement, please contact MAWA Magazine immediately. Additionally, any use of MAWA Magazine's trademarks, including the magazine's name and logo, without prior written authorization from the magazine, is strictly prohibited.

MAWA Magazine strives to showcase original and unique content, and as such, does not accept any submissions that have been previously published or that are under consideration by other publications. By submitting their work to MAWA Magazine, the author confirms that their work is original and has not been published or submitted elsewhere.

In addition, MAWA Magazine reserves the right to edit all submissions for grammar, style, and clarity, and to reject any submission that does not adhere to the magazine's standards or guidelines. The magazine also reserves the right to remove or modify any content that is deemed inappropriate or offensive, at its sole discretion.

MAWA Magazine acknowledges and respects the rights of all individuals and groups, and will not publish any content that promotes hate speech, discrimination, or any form of violence. The magazine also respects the privacy of its contributors and readers and will not share or sell any personal information to third parties without prior written consent.

By submitting their work to MAWA Magazine, the author agrees to abide by these copyright specifics and to grant the magazine the rights outlined in this statement. The author also certifies that their work is original and does not infringe on the rights of any third party. MAWA Magazine reserves the right to modify these copyright specifics at any time without prior notice.

If you have any questions or concerns regarding these copyright specifics, please contact MAWA Magazine at info@mawamag.com.

©2023 MAWA

TABLE OF CONTENTS

As the Dojo Doctor	4
Aikido Mindulness in Motion	6
My Journey in Martial Arts	9
Early Shukokai Training	11
Tai Chi the Ultimate Exercise	13
Australasian Martial Arts Hall of Fame	15
WA Kendo Renmei	19
Crossword	23
Taking Care of Your Hamstrings	24
My Home School Class	26
Breaking Through	28
Learning Karate the Japanese Way	35
Maintaining Motivation	43
Possibilities	45
The Dojo Kun	51

ASK THE DOJO DOCTOR...

Do you have a burning question about your martial arts journey but are afraid to ask? Our resident dojo doctor is on call to answer your anonymous questions. Who is the MAWA dojo doctor?
Well, they like you, will remain anonymous. But rest assured this person has a wealth of experience, knowledge and guidance to share.

Dear Dojo Doctor,
My son wants to start doing tournaments but I am worried about him getting hurt. I know there are safety measures in place but what if it is not enough?

Dear Concerned Parent,
I understand your concerns about your son's safety when participating in tournaments. While there are safety measures in place, it's important to recognise that martial arts are a contact sport and injuries can happen. However, with proper training, equipment, and supervision, the risk of serious injury can be minimised.

Before allowing your son to participate in tournaments, I recommend that you thoroughly research the tournament organisers and their safety policies. Make sure that they have proper medical personnel on site and that their equipment requirements are up to par. Additionally, ensure that your son's instructor is properly preparing him for the tournament, both mentally and physically.

It's also important to have an open and honest conversation with your son about the risks and benefits of tournament participation. Make sure he fully understands the potential for injury and that he is willing to always follow the safety precautions.

Ultimately, the decision to allow your son to take part in tournaments is a personal one that only you can make. But with proper precautions and supervision, your son can have a fun and fulfilling experience while staying safe. Remember, martial arts teaches discipline, respect, and self-defence, and participating in tournaments can be a great way for your son to showcase his skills and grow as a martial artist.

Best of luck to you and your son on this exciting journey!

Dear Dojo Doctor,
My students aren't engaging in class. Any tips?

Dear Instructor,

Thank you for reaching out. It can be frustrating when your students are not engaging in class, but there are a few things you can try to get them more involved.

First, make sure you are keeping the class interesting and dynamic. Mix up your teaching methods and try to incorporate games or challenges that will get your students excited and motivated.

Second, try to get to know your students individually. Find out what they are interested in and what motivates them, and tailor your classes to their personalities and goals.

Third, make sure you are setting clear expectations for your students. Let them know what you expect from them in terms of effort, participation, and attitude, and reward them when they meet or exceed those expectations.

Finally, consider bringing in guest instructors or holding special events to shake things up and keep your students engaged.

I hope these tips help. Good luck with your class!

ASK THE DOJO DOCTOR...

I'm a brown belt at the moment, but I don't feel like I am very technically correct with my movements. How do I go back to basics?

Dear Martial Artist,

It's great that you have recognised the need to go back to basics to improve your technique. Many practitioners, no matter their level, can benefit from revisiting the fundamentals of their art.

First, start by reviewing the basics of your art. This may include stances, footwork, strikes, blocks, and forms. Practice them slowly and deliberately, focusing on proper form and technique.

Second, seek feedback from your instructor or a trusted senior student. Ask them to watch your movements and provide feedback on areas that need improvement. Additionally, use your phone to video yourself practicing and critique your own technique.

Third, practice regularly and consistently. Set aside dedicated time to work on your basics and make it a part of your regular routine.

Fourth, consider attending workshops or seminars focused on the fundamentals of your art. These can provide a deeper understanding and new insights into the basics.

Remember, going back to basics is not a sign of weakness, but rather a sign of dedication to improving your technique. Remember, you need a strong foundation to move forward. Keep practicing and have patience with yourself as you work towards mastery.

I went to karate classes as a kid and I feel like Karate is a good thing for my child to do however they don't seem to be getting much out of it where we are now. What should I do?

Dear Parent,

I understand your concern about your child not getting much out of their karate training. I know martial arts can be very beneficial for children, but it is important to find the right dojo and instructor that will motivate and challenge your child.

Firstly, talk to your child and ask them why they are not enjoying their karate classes. Is it the instructor, the atmosphere, or the curriculum? Once you have identified the problem, you can look for a different dojo or instructor that will better suit your child's needs.

Another option is to try a different style of martial arts, such as taekwondo or judo. Each style has its own unique curriculum and teaching methods, so it is possible that your child may respond better to a different style.

It is also important to recognize that not every child is interested in martial arts. Perhaps your child prefers team sports or other activities. It is important to allow children to explore different interests and find what truly excites them.

In the end, the most important thing is to support and encourage your child. Whether they choose to continue with karate or try something new, let them know you are proud of their efforts and will always be there to support them in their pursuits.

Send your questions to info@MAWA.com with Dojo Doctor in the subject line.

AIKIDO: MINDFULNESS IN MOTION

by
Danni McCullough BSc, MPsych (Clin), Shodan WJJF Ju-Jitsu & 1st Kyu Gyokushin Ryu Aikido & Lance Spice, Shodan Gyokushin Ryu Aikido

Mindfulness in motion or moving meditation are phrase's that have been used in many academic papers to describe the Martial Art of Aikido. These phrases basically refer to the way the practitioner must calm or still their mind while their body is in motion to effectively deliver a technique.

Aikido is a relatively modern Martial Art and is considered by many as having varying effectiveness depending on the principals of the various branches. Aikido was developed by Morihei Ueshiba (1883-1969), who came to be known as O-Sensei, he had developed the art predominately from Daito ryu Aiki Jujutsu and was inspired by his studies in Zen and meditation at the Shingon School of Buddhism (Westbrook & Ratti, 2012).

Gyokushin Ryu Aikido was developed by Terumi Washizu Sensei who was trained by Minoru Mochizuki Sensei the founder of Yoseinkan Aikido and an early student of O-Sensei. The key reason behind the development of Aikido was for the Nage (receiver of the attack) to effortlessly redirect the Uke's (attacker) energy.

Our lineage of Aikido (Gyokunen Kan Aikido) was as a result of Washizu Sensei in 2022 presenting this name to Sensei Colin Niland based on his blending Aikido with other martial arts and Aikido styles in his Budo school. The name meaning Gyoku (ball like) Nen (Minoru Mochizuki's first name) and Kan school.

In delivering our Aikido syllabus we talk to the five pillars of Gyuokushin Ryu Aikido:

1. Tai Sabaki (movement)
2. Teodoki (hand escapes)
3. Atemi (striking)
4. Ukemi (falling / rolling)
5. Nigiri Gaeshi (return grasps)

While these are all equally important parts of what Aikido practitioners do, it is important to remember that the mind moves the body. "Mind moves body" in itself seems a simple concept on the surface, but the minute you start thinking about a technique to apply, you not only loose the mind / body relationship but also the Uke / Nage relationship. Both relationships require a blending or a linked fluidity. They are both symbiotic relationships that one without the other won't deliver any level of effective outcome.

Martial arts practitioners from all forms and styles will learn choreographed techniques around a set of basic principles, eventually training regularly and consistently so that the techniques become muscle memory and almost second nature. In the early stages of training students are thinking about foot placement, movement, blocking, striking, grasps locks and throws. Often these thoughts are coupled with self-judgement and other internal dialogue. In addition, trying to remember all the various aspects of techniques can lead to a lack of movement and breathing and over thinking. This ultimately impacts the delivery of the technique and results in trying to muscle the technique or failing to take the ukes Kuzushi (taking the opponents balance). The irony is that students at all levels can suffer similar failings when they feel pressure from demonstrating in front of other students or when defending attacks from senior belts.

It's within this space that Mindfulness and Aikido blend, with the practice of one set of principles working to help improve and enhance the other. Mindfulness is the practice of paying attention, on purpose, in the present moment and noticing one's thoughts, feelings, physical experiences without judgement (Kabat-Zinn, 2003). It is often paired with meditative techniques, such as deep breathing, to assist with focus and calming the nervous system and controlling the bodies "fight or flight" response. In the everyday practice of mindfulness individuals report improved sleep, lower stress levels and physiological benefits such as lower blood pressure (Brand et al., 2012; Solano-Lopez, 2018). Studies have found that practitioners of martial arts when compared to non-practitioners have significantly higher levels of mindfulness and well-being, as well as improved psychological health (Kobayashi, M.H. et al. 2020).

An example of how Mindfulness and Aikido work together can be seen in the practice of Kihonwaza (basic techniques). Kihonwaza require us to execute basic body movements, such as Tai Sabaki and Naegiri Kaeshi, coordinating movement and timing with an Uke. This requires the student to adapt a state of Mushin (the mind is alert but empty of thoughts) and Musubi (the state of mental and physical connection between training partners). The student's attention must be in the present and attuned with their internal experiences and external environment, creating the basic state of Mindfulness. Secondly, while conducting movement in repetitive and flowing motion, students are encouraged to breathe and activate their Ki (inner energy held at the centre of the body). This has the effect of lowering the heart rate, reducing cortisol levels and further grounding the student in the present, potentially deepening their meditative state.

The final and possibly most challenging element of Aikido and Mindfulness practice is the student learning to adapt a mindset of non-judgement. This task requires us to have the ability to acknowledge when our inner experience shifts from the present focus to unhelpful thoughts and feelings i.e., embarrassment or frustration at our performance. We then need to intentionally, without negative judgement, move our mind back to the present – in this case, our breathing and movement.

The benefits of this practice are exponential, influencing everything from our ability to improve technical expertise to learning how to manage our emotions and the challenges that we all face in daily life.

As research continues into the physical and psychological benefits of modern Mindfulness and Aikido practice, it's important to look back and remember the words of Morihei Ueshiba – "Master the divine techniques of the Art of Peace and no enemy will dare to challenge you". It is with the promise of finding the balance of calm and fortitude that O-Sensei invites us to step onto the mats and discover for ourselves the path of the Budo.

Gyokunen Kan Aikido
www.ommabudo.com
Sensei Colin Niland
Sandan Gyokushin Ryu Aikido - 0405946661

References

Brand, S., Holsboer-Trachsler, E., Naranjo, J. R., & Schmidt, S. (2012). Influence of mindfulness practice on cortisol and sleep in long-term and short-term meditators. Neuropsychobiology, 65(3), 109-118.

Kabat-Zinn, J. (2003). Mindfulness-based stress reduction (MBSR). Constructivism in the Human Sciences, 8(2), 73.

Miyata, H., Kobayashi, D., Sonoda, A., Motoike, H., & Akatsuka, S. (2020). Mindfulness and psychological health in practitioners of Japanese martial arts: a cross-sectional study. BMC sports science, medicine and rehabilitation, 12, 1-10.

Solano Lopez, A. L. (2018). Effectiveness of the mindfulness-based stress reduction program on blood pressure: a systematic review of literature. Worldviews on Evidence-Based Nursing, 15(5), 344-352.

Westbrook, A., & Ratti, O. (2012). Aikido and the dynamic sphere: An illustrated introduction. Tuttle Publishing.

My Journey in Martial Arts

by Chris McVay

I want to share my personal story about how martial arts have positively impacted my life. My struggles began when I was just 13 years old. I was jumped by a group of older teenagers who left me for dead in the street. I never lost consciousness, and the experience left me shaken and vulnerable.

I was an average student, but my athletic ability set me apart from others. I excelled at any activity involving upper body strength. I was good at high jump, discus, javelin, and shot-put. I was always quite strong. People often picked on me for having long, curly hair, and times were different in the 80s and 90s.

I began my ninjutsu journey as a means to defend myself against bigger opponents if needed. The club was a new one, run by a friend of my cousin from his old school in a place called Whitley Bay. Then it moved to North Shields. This was all in North Tyneside in the UK, and I stayed there for several years, gaining new friends, learning new techniques and passing a few gradings.

Eventually, I moved on to kickboxing and fought in a few tournaments. I even drove eight hours south to fight and then drove back eight hours immediately after. Although I didn't get much sleep, I stayed with kickboxing long enough to earn a black belt. My instructor also taught freestyle karate at the same dojo, and I was surprised to be welcomed to his karate class as a black belt too.

In 1994, my parents emigrated to New Zealand, and I could not take the club with me. I found another ninjutsu club and trained there for a while. Unfortunately, I later found out that my instructor was a hired killer who did a job, got caught, and then hung himself. The police asked questions of us all, but we knew nothing.

That was the end of that club. This was all a big shock to us as he seemed nice, the club was set up well and we trained hard the old school way.

I met a girl, and we moved to Australia a year later. She wasn't into martial arts back then, so yet again, I had another little break from it. Two years later I joined another ninjutsu club. This time, I was determined to stay with it and finally achieved my black belt after a few years. However, the training became more sporadic, and clubs were closing or moving to different areas, so I took a break.

I tried Taekwondo, but it didn't suit me. I graded as a yellow belt within three months and sparred with blue, brown, and black belts, but I found it wasn't for me. I left and started my journey in Aikido, which I have been practicing for six years now.

My passion for martial arts has never faded, and I recently started practicing Aikido with Sensei Dave in Port Kennedy. Aikido has been a fantastic addition to my journey, especially as someone who has faced challenges throughout my life. It's also great for those who may be a little hesitant to start a martial art due to their body shape or age.

Aikido has been a game-changer for me, especially as I get older and my body is not as strong as it used to be. The training is at my own pace, and I enjoy the company of the people there who support each other and help each other succeed. I believe this will be my last martial art in this life, as it fits just right with any injury I may have had. They work around what I'm capable of and always think positively.

Martial arts have taught me discipline, self-defence, and self-awareness. They have helped me overcome my struggles and have given me a purpose. I hope my story can inspire others to start their own martial arts journey so they can experience the benefits it can bring.

Currently, I have made it to brown belt and I am excited to continue my journey to achieve a black belt and beyond. I would love to invite others to join me at Aikido Port Kennedy and be a part of my story.

Early Shukokai Training
by Sensei Don Godwin

How many of us remember our first karate class? Although I can well remember watching one before I joined the club and can picture every detail of the dojo, the first few weeks were a blend of memories.

My best friend had started a month before, and I clearly recall we were standing in my backyard when he asked me to guess what he was doing. Naturally, I had no idea, and when he told me he had taken up karate, I was enthralled. With my mom's permission, I went along to watch a class and straightaway decided it was for me. To this day, I have never forgotten Mom's edict – "if you start this, don't come back to me and say you want to quit." (some 25 years later she would ask me when I planned to stop training!)

I would like to say my friend continued with me on the journey, but he stopped shortly afterwards (although we are still friends!) and I settled into training with an Indian boy a few years younger, but far more experienced. Initially I was very tense, and he constantly berated me for jamming rather than deflecting with my blocks. My arms were black with bruises, but amazingly, I continued.

Like almost everyone, when I started, I did not know that there were different styles. My club practised Shukokai, and although Shukokai had been formed in 1949, I believe that my Sensei, Des Botes, and senior students like Sandy McCellan and Graham Campbell had trained in other styles. From what I understand, Sensei Kimura would run a course and entice other stylists to join Shukokai by getting them to hold a pad while he hit it. He amazed everyone with his phenomenal power and drew students in by offering to teach them how to do the same.

Sensei Kimura

Unlike most students, I did not initially have ambitions to be a black belt. I just accepted that there were higher grades: Sandy was a brown belt and Graham was green, and the rest of us, as I recall, were white belts. I had no idea there were such things as gradings, but that was about to change!

Sensei advised us that a Japanese black belt would be 'in residence', for around two months. There was a course fee, which may have been quite steep; but I persuaded my parents to let me attend.

The Japanese black belt was none other than Sensei Kimura. The thing that struck me in the first class was the influx of new black belts, and although I didn't know it at the time, I later discovered they had come up from South Africa especially to train with him.

Prior to the course, my techniques were delivered with an emphasis on power, from a deep stance and a hollow back. (a curve at the base of the spine) Sensei introduced me to the 'double twist' – where the hip was pulled back and then thrust forward, propelling the punching hand faster than the muscles in the arm could do on their own. In fact, the arm was relaxed until impact. The stance was slightly higher, and the back foot was turned inwards to 45 degrees.

We did a lot of gykazuki, Sensei's theory being that indoctrination in one technique would flow to the rest. We were also introduced to the concept that impact = (mass x acceleration)^2. Meaning that although the weight of the fist was finite, any increase in speed would have an exponential effect.

We also did loads of pad work. Sensei Kimura had brought impact pads with him and each of the visiting black belts and adult students were invited to try out his punch. From the looks on their faces, the impact went straight through. I was relieved to be excused because I was too young. There were also lots of katas, including Tensho (After all, the course was directed at black belt level).

> The origins of Tensho can be traced back to the Naha-te style developed in the late 19th and early 20th centuries by Chojun Miyagi, who is credited with creating the kata following a trip to China in 1915.
> Tensho is designed to develop fluidity and circular movements in the practitioner's technique. It also emphasises breathing and the control of one's centre of gravity in order to gain superior balance and power in their movements.
> The name Tensho means "rotating hands." The kata is performed with a series of circular movements, with the hands rotating in a variety of ways. These movements are designed to help the practitioner learn to generate power through circular motions and to maintain their balance while doing so.

There was a grading at the end of the course. This was before the introduction of the extra grades we have today, so a white belt was 6th kyu. I was going on holiday shortly before the course ended and optimistically thought I might miss the grading (I was terrified), but Sensei arranged a special grading for me and Lionel Marinus (now 9th Dan), who was heading back to Johannesburg. Sensei Lionel was going for 2nd Dan and of course he passed, to great applause from the group. Sensei Kimura then turned to go out, leaving me to think that I had failed. Then he turned round and pointed at me,
"You - Little One," he said, pause, "5th kyu!"
More applause! I was pretty pleased with myself.

Don Godwin (5th Dan Shukokai) instructs In Karrinyup. He has been training with Shukokai for over 50 years and teaching for 40. Shukokai is a fast, practical style and female friendly.
 Contact Don on 0450 772 846 to arrange 2 weeks free training.

TAI CHI THE ULTIMATE EXERCISE

Tai Chi: The Ultimate Exercise

Tai Chi, it's been around for centuries. So why is it still relatively unknown, and how can moving slowly be good exercise for you?

Tai Chi is a set of movements that are performed slowly in order to promote good health. Originating in China centuries ago, this ancient art literally translated means the "Supreme Ultimate" and its main purpose was specifically designed for self-defence in the martial arts.

Martial artists of that period were constantly in search of a fighting style that was unbeatable or the "ultimate" fighting style. What they discovered was that the more relaxed you were during a fight, your thoughts were clear and free from emotional anger thus, being able to respond to attacks more appropriately giving you the upper hand over an opponent whose judgement was clouded by anger.

So in order to train the body to be more relaxed during fighting, they practised techniques slowly. This relaxed the muscles and prevented them from tensing up, it slowed their breathing down and lowered their heart rate. They discovered other benefits - the overall health of practitioners improved when practicing this type of training.

Weight Loss

Fitness professionals will recommend higher intensity exercises, such as running to burn more calories faster. A typical one-hour Tai Chi session can burn somewhere between 280-300 calories. Simply put, if you're moving, you're burning calories. If you're burning calories, you're contributing to weight loss.

Fitness

Tai Chi gets you to work on special breathing techniques that help cultivate your 'Qi' or 'Chi' energy throughout your body. Any kind of breath work is essentially using your heart and lungs, which are the primary organs used to improve your cardio-respiratory system.

Stress Relief, Focus and Concentration

Tai Chi requires you to move slowly and keep your body relaxed. Moving in such a way gives you the sensation of what can be best described as 'moving meditation'. When moving in a meditative like state, your mind must concentrate as well as be totally aware of every minute move.

Ailments and Diseases

As mentioned earlier, Tai Chi movements are designed to cultivate Qi to flow freely throughout the body. If there is an interruption to this 'flow', this is believed to be the cause of sickness, both mental and physical. Tai Chi aims to balance the flow of Qi.

Energy Levels

After a Tai Chi session, you will feel totally relaxed and energised. A combination of mind and body exercise, you are left feeling good about yourself, not only physically, but mentally as well.

Confidence and Relationships

When you feel good about yourself, you will discover a new sense of confidence which can lead you into interacting with people around you more positively.

Tai Chi should be practised with full heartedness and sincerity. It is a harmonious combination of art and exercise that provides a deeper level of self knowledge and spiritual harmony. With constant practice, one will soon find balance and understand their place in the universe.

Sam Sujatna
Head Instructor
Email:
info@perthtaichi.com.au
Mobile: 0415 165 908

Unveiling Excellence
Australasian Martial Arts Hall of Fame
A Weekend of Martial Arts Celebration in Sydney
2023
by
Colin Wee

The Australasian Martial Arts Hall of Fame (AMAHOF) is a unique organisation recognising and celebrating the achievements of influential martial artists in the Australasian region. What sets AMAHOF apart is that it is independent, not-for-profit, volunteer-run, and apolitical. President of AMAHOF Ed Scharrer frequently emphasises this group was "started by martial artists, for martial artists." Since its inception in 1996, the organisation has been committed to promoting ethical standards, fostering fellowship, and upholding teaching excellence throughout the martial arts community.

The annual Presentation and Gala Event is the highlight of AMAHOF's calendar. This grand event brings together martial artists, friends, family, and supporters to witness the induction of new members into the Hall of Fame. The event serves as a platform to highlight the remarkable achievements of existing members, facilitating networking opportunities amongst industry peers, and hosting an evening of entertainment and celebration for the martial arts community.

The 2022 AMAHOF gala event held in Perth in September was a resounding success. Guest-of-Honour Mr. David Kelly, Minister for Youth from the WA Government, graced the occasion, adding prestige to the event. The Taiko On drummers, led by inductee Simon Vanyai, delivered a powerful performance that ignited the festivities, setting the tone for an unforgettable evening.

Following the hiatus caused by the COVID-19 pandemic, the 2022 gala saw the induction of a significant number of individuals for the years 2020, 2021, and 2022. Among the esteemed martial artists honoured were Peter Wong, Sean Allen, Alan Pond (Posthumously), Wayne Spear, Victor Stuart, Tom Bellamy, Diana LaTorre, Wayne Swanton, Lionel Daley, Lincoln Harris, Matt Geister, Benjamin Pollet, Paul Veldman, Andrew Coatsworth, Colin Wee, Dean Woodhams, Peter Hunt, Simon Vanyai, Tom Johnson, and Vince Cordeiro.

AMAHOF President Ed Scharrer
and attendees at the AMAHOF AGM 2022

Looking ahead, AMAHOF's upcoming Presentation and Gala Event in Sydney over the weekend of 18-20th August 2023 promises to be an even bigger celebration.

The festivities kick off on Friday afternoon with an Annual General Meeting, where board members come together to discuss the future of AMAHOF and its initiatives. Following the meeting, a special 'Meet and Greet' session is organised, offering attendees the opportunity to interact with soon-to-be inducted members. This casual gathering fosters connections and camaraderie among participants, creating a warm and welcoming atmosphere right from the start.

The following day, a diverse range of workshops and demonstrations awaits eager participants. Led by each esteemed AMAHOF inductee, these seminars delve into various martial art topics, catering to practitioners of all levels. From exploring traditional applications and honing weapon skills to mastering self-defence techniques and ground fighting strategies, these sessions provide a wealth of knowledge and practical insights. Regardless of one's martial arts background, there will be something valuable to learn and apply to their own practice.

Dean Woodhams and student

AMAHOF President Ed Scharrer

The Australasian Martial Arts Hall of Fame (AMAHOF) is a unique organisation recognising and celebrating the achievements of influential martial artists in the Australasian region. What sets AMAHOF apart is that it is independent, not-for-profit, volunteer-run, and apolitical.

Peter Hunt

Colin Wee

Undoubtedly, the highlight of the weekend is the prestigious gala awards ceremony. This elegant black-tie affair serves as the crowning moment of the event, formalizing the induction of new members into the Hall of Fame. The ceremony also serves as a platform to recognise significant milestones and key developments among existing members. As attendees gather in their finest attire, the ambiance exudes glamour and sophistication, adding an air of prestige to the proceedings. Witnessing the heartfelt speeches and seeing the honourees take their rightful place among martial arts legends creates a truly unforgettable experience for all in attendance.

The event transcends the glitz and glamour of the gala awards ceremony. The morning following the ceremony, prominent instructors take the stage to lead a series of seminars that close off the immersive journey for attendees. These sessions are a rare opportunity for participants to train under renowned master instructors, delving into advanced techniques and refining skills. This invaluable opportunity should not be missed by any enthusiast seeking to expand their skills and knowledge.

Nominations for induction into the Hall of Fame are open to all who have made significant contributions to the development of martial arts across Australasia. This includes individuals who have excelled in their chosen martial art style, are noted for their community involvement, or who have demonstrated a dedication to promoting martial art values and ethics. The nomination can be submitted until the cut-off date in March of each year, with more information available at https://www.amahof.asn.au/.

Sean Allen

Make sure to mark your calendar and prepare for the unforgettable AMAHOF Presentation and Gala Event in Sydney in August 2023. The weekend celebration promises camaraderie, entertainment, and an opportunity to honour and celebrate excellence in martial arts.

Participants are taken down with a variety of locks and holds under Sean Allen's watchful eye.

Wayne Spears

Author Colin Wee has practiced three martial arts systems over three continents in the past 40 years. Colin was inducted into AMAHOF in 2020, and currently serves as a Board member. He's recently published a book titled Breaking Through: The Secrets of Bassai Dai Kata available on Amazon.

Ramon Lawrence performing Tamaya Ryu Iaido, Chojo.

The Western Australian Kendo Renmei
Kendo, Iaido and Jodo

The Western Australian Kendo Renmei (WAKR) covers three martial arts: Kendo, Iaido and Jodo. We are part of the Australian Kendo Renmei (AKR) which is part of the Federation of International Kendo (FIK).

Kendo - The Way of the Sword (Ken: sword + Do: way). Kendo is one of Japan's oldest martial arts, and the one most closely associated with the Samurai. The concept of kendo is to discipline the human spirit through the principles of the katana (Japanese sword). While Kendo has gained popularity as a sport, the principles of the warrior remain evident. It is suitable for both men and women, who compete and train together. The concept of Kendo is to discipline the human character through the application of the principles of the Katana (Japanese Sword).

Iaido - Way of mental presence and immediate reaction. Iaido encompasses hundreds of styles of swordsmanship, all of which subscribe to non-combative aims and purposes. Iaido is an intrinsic form of Japanese modern budo. Iaido is performed solo as an issue of kata, executing changed strategies against single or various fanciful rivals. Every kata starts and finishes with the sword sheathed. Notwithstanding sword method, it obliges creative ability and fixation to keep up the inclination of a genuine battle and to keep the kata new.

Jodo - Way of the short staff. Jodo is strongly focused upon defence against the Japanese sword. Jodo training involves the study of basic movements and kata prearranged attack and defence movements. As with other Budo arts, Jodo is designed to preserve the ancient combat techniques, but with the aim of helping the modern student to achieve control over mind and body through repeated practice.

A Brief History

To the best of our knowledge, Kendo was first practiced in Western Australia in 1978 when a Japanese high school exchange student named Owada Tsukasa (a 2nd dan in Kendo) first taught Kendo to Brian Brestovac, Dennis Brestovac and Robert Mateljan. The first lesson being in a backyard of the Brestovac household. Kendo armours was difficult to get at that time, but we managed to buy two sets and borrow a set to practice with. In late 1978, Owada Tsukasa returned to Japan.

In 1979, Robert Mateljan contacted Maeda sensei, who was teaching at the local Japanese school and was a 5th Dan in Kendo. Brian Brestovac and Robert Mateljan started training with him and other students that joined (below picture with Maeda sensei in the centre in white).

Maeda sensei returned to Japan in late 1979 and again we had no instructor. Some of the group tried to keep going but eventually disbanded, and Kendo was not practiced in Western Australia for several years.

In 1984 Adrian Baird, a 1st Dan Kendoka from England, visited Western Australia to see his sister. He trained with Brian Brestovac and Rob Mateljan for a few months and encouraged the formation of a Kendo club, which was called "WA Budo". In 1985, contact was made with a club training in Fremantle under Kuzu Uchino, a 2nd Dan in Kendo.

The formation of the Western Australian Kendo Renmei (WAKR) was founded on the 21st of September 1986, through the Fremantle club. The first president was Andrew Bennison, secretary was Mike Parsonage, treasure was Russell Lawrence and the development officer was Ramon Lawrence. The club changed several venues but finally settled in 1988 in Canningvale, and adopted the name the "Budokan Academy" which became the long-time headquarters of the WAKR. In 1988, the WA Budo club joined the WAKR. Over the years, several clubs have joined and today the WAKR has approximately 150 members.

In 1990, Ramon Lawrence co-founded the WA branch of the "Seitei Gata Ryu Iaido" with Jerry Yee. Iaido in Western Australia was born. Iaido, as part of the WAKR, has developed into one of the most advanced and successful groups practicing in Australia. Ramon Lawrence also served as the president of the WAKR for over 26 years. In 1991, Owada Tsukasa, the original exchange student that started Kendo in Western Australia, returned. By this time he was 5th Dan in Iaido and 4th Dan in Kendo. He stayed for two years and helped develop both Iaido and Kendo.

Also in 1991, the WAKR hosted the first Australian Kendo Championship (AKC) in Western Australia, at Sacred Hearts College, Sorento. A delegation of 14 highly ranked Kendo sensei, under the leadership of Takeshi Matsushima sensei, came from Japan to run seminars and assist with the AKC. At this 16th Australian Kendo Championship, Robert Mateljan came first in the Kyu grade individual competition and so was the first Western Australian to win a Kendo event at a national level.

In March 1993, the first WAKR commenced Jodo training at the Budokan Academy under Derek Woodhouse, 4th Dan Jodo. Thus, the WAKR had the full complement of martial arts under its banner – Kendo, Iaido and Jodo. The WA Budo club changes its name to the Go Shin Kai Kendo club and was training at the University of WA.

> Current clubs that are part of the WAKR: Kendo: Sukura Kendo club, GoShinKai Kendo club, Murdoch Kendo club, UWA Kendo club, West Coast Kendo club.
> Iaido and Jodo: Budokan Academy, Ju Go Kan, Southwest Budokan, Bunbury Budokan, Perth Japanese Sword School, Seibukan.

In 1997, the Murdoch University Club was founded by Chris Graham, who trained at the ANU club in Canberra and then in Sydney. The Murdoch club has had great success and continues today with Kendo training. In 1999, Chiharu Fukumoto moved to Perth and trained at the Go Shin Kai Kendo club. He had trained in WA before but left to go back to Japan and upon his return started Kendo training here in WA. Chiharu Fukumoto, then established the Sukura kendo club that trains at the Perth Modern High school. In 2023, he was successful in obtaining his 7th Dan in Japan and is currently the highest ranked Western Australian Kendoka.

Southwest Iaido and Jodo: The Busselton club came into existence in 1998 and only taught Iaido. About three years later, another dojo opened in Dunsborough. About that time tuition in Jodo began. Several years later, the Busselton Dojo closed, and the Dunsborough Dojo continued. Training commenced in Margaret River about 10 years ago at the MR Karate club premises. Both Dunsborough and Margaret River Dojos are part of South West Budokan with its parent Dojo in Perth. Training is ongoing, with strong and enthusiastic membership.

In 2010, Dong Yeol Lim came to Western Australia and started training with the Go Shin Kai Kendo club, started the Sung Moon Kendo Club teaching adults and children. He has had to leave WA and now resides in Tasmania; however, the club continues through the instruction of William Yoo 5th Dan, and is now the UWA Kendo club.

The Bunbury Budokan club trains Seitei Iaido and Zen Nippon Kendo Renmei Jodo. In March 2017, Terri Gallear took over the club. They train once a week and visit the Budokan Academy regularly for seminars.

The Progress of Kendo, Iaido and Jodo in Australia, A History of the Australian Kendo Renmei, by Ron Bennett and Bob brown. https://wakr.asn.au

Peter Woolmer and Ben Wood training Jodo. Ben Wood attacks with the sword while Peter Woolmer moves and counter strikes with the Jo.

Kendo training in Western Australia. Brian Brestovac doing a "Do" cut (across the stomach) of an opponent.

CROSSWORD

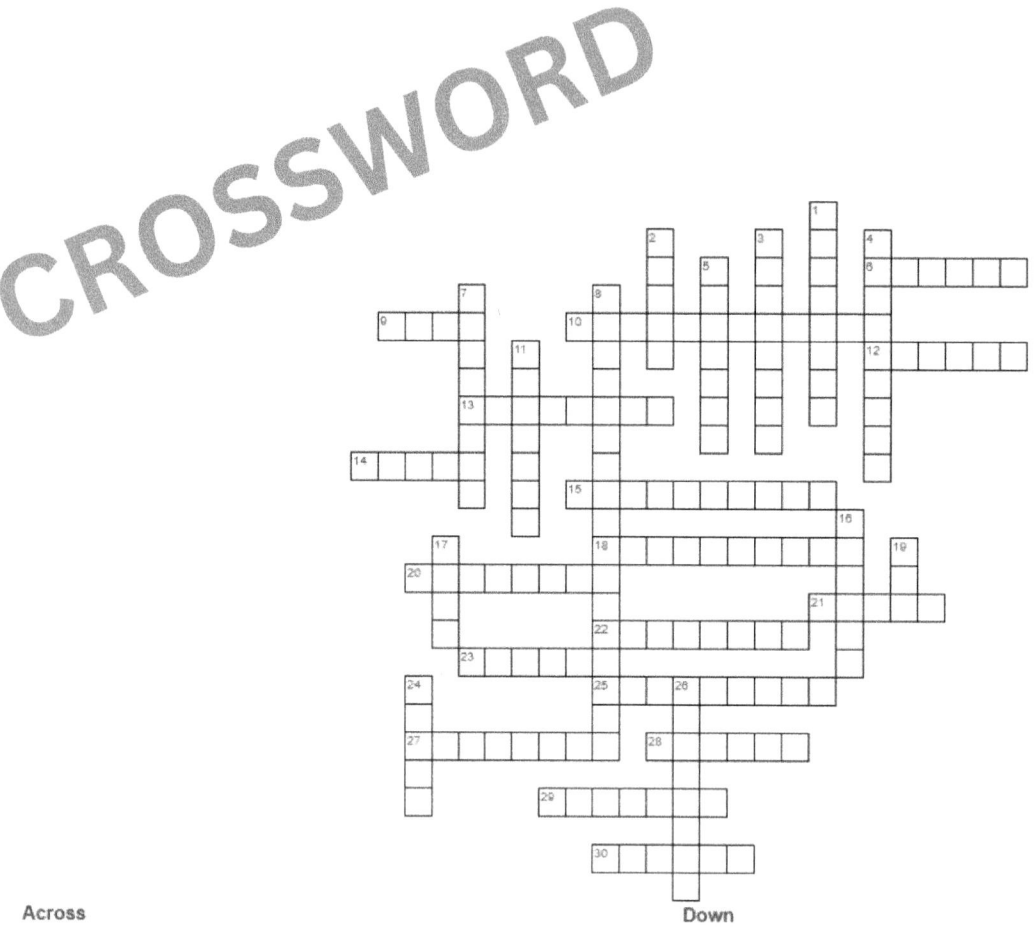

Across

6 Japanese martial art focused on using an opponent's energy against them (6 letters)
9 Philippine martial art that emphasizes weapons training (4 letters)
10 Thai martial art that uses swords, staffs, and other weapons (11 letters)
12 French martial art known for its kicks and footwork (6 letters)
13 Brazilian martial art that combines dance, acrobatics, and music (8 letters)
14 Chinese martial art that emphasizes forms and acrobatics (5 letters)
15 Ancient Greek martial art that allowed both striking and grappling (10 letters)
18 Bruce Lee's martial art philosophy that emphasises fluidity and adaptability (11 letters)
20 Combat sport from Thailand known for its striking techniques (8 Letters)
21 Indonesian martial art that utilizes strikes, grappling, and weapons (5 letters)
22 Japanese martial art focused on throws, joint locks, and chokes (8 letters)
23 Chinese martial art known for its slow, graceful movements (6 letters)
25 Korean martial art known for its high kicks and fast footwork (9 letters)
27 Japanese martial art developed by ninja for espionage and assassination (8 letters)
28 Japanese martial art known for its striking techniques (7 letters)
29 Filipino martial art that uses sticks and other weapons (7 letters)
30 Chinese martial art that emphasises fluid movements and kicks (6 letters)

Down

1 Style of karate developed by Gichin Funakoshi (8 letters)
2 Russian martial art that combines grappling and striking techniques (5 letters)
3 A practitioner of karate (8 letters)
4 Korean martial art similar to karate (9 letters)
5 Cambodian martial art that utilizes punches, kicks, and grappling (7 letters)
7 Chinese martial art known for close-range fighting and quick punches (8 letters)
8 Brazilian martial art focused on grappling and ground fighting (18 letters)
11 Korean martial art focused on joint locks and throws (7 letters)
16 Sport that involves punching and footwork (6 letters)
17 Japanese martial art focused on throws and grappling (4 letters)
19 Mixed martial arts, a combat sport that incorporates various martial arts styles (3 letters)
24 Japanese martial art that uses bamboo swords and protective gear (5 letters)
26 Israeli martial art developed for self-defense and real-world combat situations (8 letters)

23

Taking Care of Hamstrings

Hamstring injuries are a common problem for martial artists, especially those who take part in high-intensity training. These injuries can be painful, debilitating, and can take months to heal, so it's important to take preventative measures to avoid them

First, it's important to understand what the hamstrings are and how they can be damaged. The hamstrings are a group of three muscles located at the back of the thigh that work together to flex and extend the leg. These muscles are responsible for movements such as running, jumping, and kicking. Hamstring injuries often occur when these muscles are stretched beyond their limit, causing small tears in the muscle fibres.

To prevent hamstring injuries, stretch and warm up properly before class. This can include a combination of dynamic and static stretching exercises. Dynamic stretching involves movements that are similar to those used in class, such as high kicks and leg swings. Static stretching involves holding a stretch for a period of time, such as the classic hamstring stretch where you reach for your toes while standing or seated on the ground.

Besides stretching, warming up before class is crucial. This can include jogging, jumping jacks, or other light cardio exercises to increase blood flow and warm up the muscles. It's also important to gradually increase the intensity of your training session to avoid sudden strain on the muscles.

Another way to prevent hamstring injuries is to make sure you are practicing proper form and technique. This means paying attention to your body and avoiding movements that cause pain or discomfort. It's also important to listen to your body and take breaks when necessary.

If you experience a hamstring injury, seek treatment right away. Ignoring the injury or trying to push through the pain can lead to more serious damage and an even longer recovery time.

The right treatment for a hamstring injury can include rest, ice, compression, and elevation (RICE). This means taking a break from training, applying ice to the affected area, using compression bandages to reduce swelling, and elevating the injured leg to reduce blood flow to the area.

Ignoring the injury or trying to push through the pain can lead to more serious damage and an even longer recovery time.

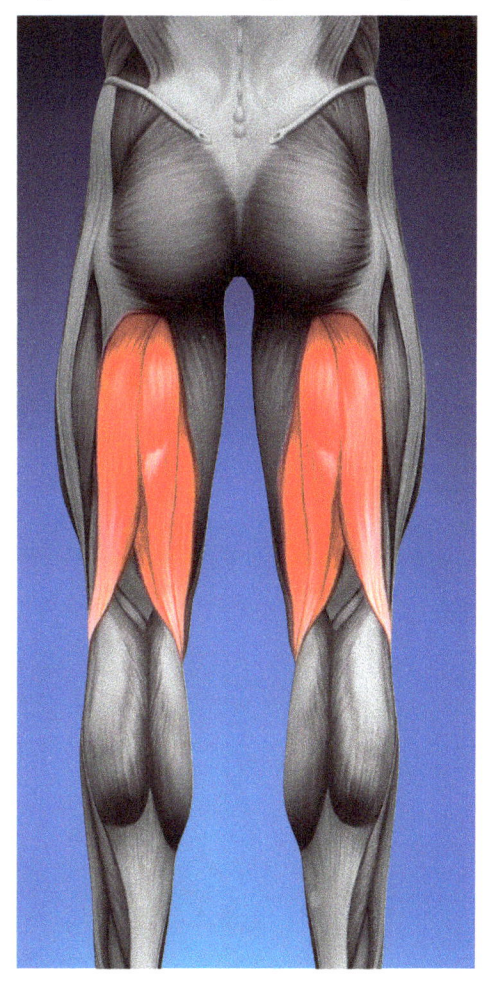

Physical therapy can be helpful in the recovery process. A trained professional can guide you through targeted exercises to help strengthen the affected muscles and improve flexibility. They can also advise you on how to gradually return to training without further injuring the hamstring.

In severe cases, surgery may be needed to repair the damaged muscles. However, this is usually only necessary in cases where the injury is very severe or the muscle has completely torn.

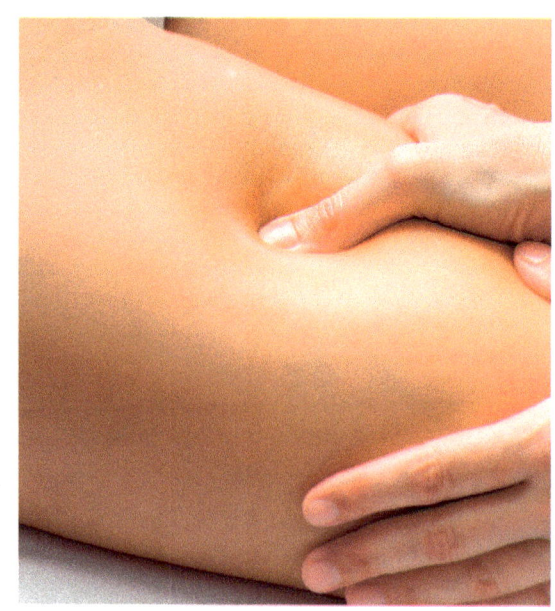

Overall, preventing hamstring injuries should be a top priority for martial artists. By taking proper precautions and seeking treatment.

Finally, it's important to incorporate rest and recovery into your training routine. This means taking days off when needed and getting enough sleep and proper nutrition to aid in muscle recovery.

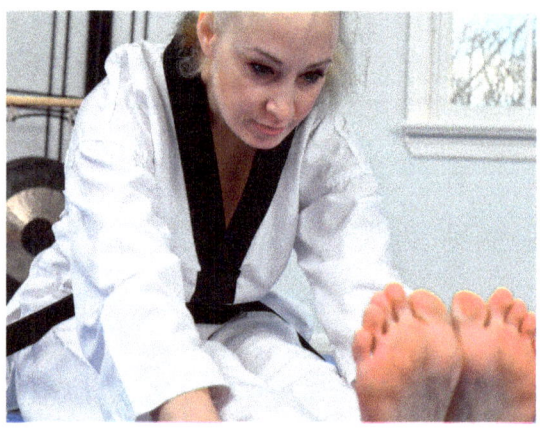

Hamstring injuries can be a frustrating setback for martial artists, but with proper stretching, warming up, technique, and rest, they can largely be prevented. By taking these preventative measures, martial artists can continue to focus on their training and progress.

Why I Love my Home School Class

by Iain Humphreys

I've been running a Karate dojo in Mandurah since 2010. I love it, although the challenge of keeping the students interested in continuing their journey in martial arts alongside keeping the traditional art-form quality is always a bit of a balance.

Running my own business was always something I had wanted to do, however the reality, as I'm sure some of you know, is far from easy, both financially and mentally. So, when I was approached five years ago, by a mum of a 10-year-old that was home-schooled about whether I would teach him karate in a one-on-one session I agreed, thinking that this would be another avenue of raising revenue.

The one-on-one class quickly evolved into a small class of five students that I ran from my local park. The home-school community is quite large in Western Australia and resources to help support these children can be limited at best and appallingly unprofessional at worst.

Most home-schooled kids are individuals that either don't quite fit into the public education system because of personal viewpoints or have physical and emotional needs that are not provided by the public educational system. Either way, the guardians of these children have curriculum expectations put upon them that the governing educational body requires to be met.

I now run a home-school class every Thursday morning from one of my normal karate venues. We can fluctuate wildly in numbers but regularly average 15 students. I use the home-school class as a step up for kids to becoming full training members in the main dojo, something that has proved extremely fruitful in the past and continues to be so.

Things I have learned in running a home-school class:

- **Don't run it like a normal, strict martial arts class.**

These kids do not always do what they are asked and lean towards doing what they want, learn to guide rather than discipline. They come around to more disciplined behaviour once they trust you.

- **Keep it casual**.

I play more focus, fun games rather than sticking to pure traditional martial arts. The more they laugh, the more relaxed they feel. They'll keep returning to enjoy the atmosphere if you do this correctly. Also, I don't hold gradings or insist on wearing karate gis, casual across the board.

- **Don't expect to make lots of money.**

This really covers most martial arts clubs, but especially for home-schooled classes. The financial benefits come because students keep returning, then request becoming normal club members. I charge a low fee for each class rather than a monthly or term-based fee structure, as I do in my main classes. This gives the parents more flexibility.

- **Embrace the differences.**

Running this class has made me a better teacher, mainly because I had to learn to compromise my art-form for a little while to gain the changes in the kids. Seeing a little 7-year-old who struggles to leave their mum's side without crying on their first visit progress to confidently performing 'head and thigh tap' drills with new students is more uplifting than I can tell you.

At the end of the day, I'll probably not produce star pupils that shine on the mat using stunning fixation and beautifully strong stances from my home-school class. They may never defend themselves against multiple opponents or win fights in octagon cages. What I will produce, however, are kids, teenagers and eventually adults that have the self-confidence, self-belief and courage to navigate society as individuals with good morals. This is one benefit of practising traditional martial arts.

By the way, that young 10-year-old who started the whole thing is a 1st kyu brown belt now and will attempt his Shodan black belt in the next couple of years.

Iain Humphreys
Kofukan Karate Mandurah
https://karatemandurah.com

BREAKING THROUGH
The Secrets of Bassai Dai Kata

Colin Wee

AVAILABLE WHERE ALL GOOD BOOKS ARE SOLD!

Breaking Through
My First Martial Arts Book by Colin Wee

I've done it. I've published a martial arts book! And boy, was it a journey. I thought I'd share my experience with you. Be warned: it wasn't an easy ride.

I started writing before the COVID pandemic and finished most of the first draft of the manuscript that first year. While everyone else complained about being locked up at home and organising coffee sessions over Zoom calls, I took on this mammoth task. If I'd known how much work it was going to be, I might have reconsidered.

Writing the manuscript itself took about a year, and then came the task of submitting it to the publisher, re-writing, and editing the document. Plus, we had to commission cover artwork and arrange several photo shoots to gather images for the applications presented. Not to mention the back-and-forth emails with my focus group to gather their feedback on the developing material.

You may ask why I wrote a book. Well, it could have been I wanted approval from my teachers and seniors, or maybe I'd been pestered enough over the years to publish something. Or you could simply say I was ready to tell a story that really began a long, long time ago.

I'd actually written another manuscript around twenty years back tentatively titled "Fighting Heaven and Earth." Heaven and Earth is the first of our Taekwondo forms. That manuscript started as a resource to map out applications within the Taekwondo pattern set. But, upon finishing it, I realised it wasn't the book I had intended to write. It prompted more questions than it provided answers. It was more like a lament of what I didn't know.

Although it seemed like a waste of effort, that manuscript actually became a roadmap for us. It set us on the path to develop the distinct training methodology we use in our school today. We call this distinct training methodology the JDK Method. This is the foundation around which all else has been built. I say "us," "our," and "we" because the collaboration between me and my black belts is a fundamental part of the JDK training environment. Without their feedback and participation, the JDK Method might not exist.

Will Just & Colin Wee

In the award-winning Breaking Through: The Secrets of Bassai Dai Kata, Master Colin Wee explores applications and concepts extrapolated from Bassai Dai kata. Bassai Dai is one of a group of forms which transcends cultures and styles through traditional martial arts originating from Okinawa to Japan to Korea. Inspired by this kata, Wee's twelve combative applications are compelling and practical as lessons for martial artists who train using fixed set patterns. More than 200 photos clearly illustrate not only hard-style striking but also effective, soft-style principles, traps and takedowns generally overlooked in modern martial arts training such as Karate and Taekwondo. The insights gleaned from Breaking Through encourage readers to explore body structure and mechanics and demonstrate how picture-perfect techniques become combat-oriented defense strategies. Masters of old depended on these principles, strategies and wisdom for their very lives, and transmitted them to their students through kata. As a student of the martial arts for more than four decades, Wee accepts the responsibilities of the originators of Bassai to pass this knowledge to all who would study it with him. Readers need not know Bassai Dai, as Wee's methods can be applied to any form in any style to inspire and enrich patterns training beyond simplistic rote, choreographed routines.

When the idea of writing a book resurfaced in the spring of 2019, my school had just spent a year and a half focused on the practice of one kata: Bassai Dai. Even though we're a Taekwondo school, we incorporate legacy classical Karate forms into our syllabus, and we often do a deep dive on specific forms. Bassai Dai seemed like the perfect subject since a wide range of Okinawan, Japanese, and Korean stylists practice the pattern. The depth of material we had gathered and developed about the form seemed promising. We found the irony of a Taekwondo instructor publishing a Karate book as a chapter in the already compelling story of Bassai Dai somewhat amusing.

The various COVID-19 lockdowns in Western Australia and the hard border erected in 2020 were a blessing in disguise for the new book. I had plenty of time to write while keeping fit, working from home, cooking for my family, and enjoying game nights and movies. Putting my thoughts down onto a page had a lovely, meditative quality. Of course, it didn't make up for the lack of training partners, but it was a fine use of that unfortunate downtime.

Breaking Through: The Secrets of Bassai Dai Kata isn't your straight-up martial arts picture book. I initially contemplated illustrating the applications with the help of a manga artist. Manga has an amazing kinetic quality, and its ability to establish the presence of both the protagonist and the antagonist is next level. But the idea quickly fizzled as each page had to be drawn by hand and, since I have no real artistic skills, the cost per hour for an artist was more than I could afford. Although the idea was awesome and would produce a book most unique in the field of martial arts books, I had to put it in the "too hard basket."

Master Colin Wee with Road Trippers and students at Marudo Ryu Karate.

So, picture this: I have written a book. And I am feeling pretty chuffed with myself. I mean, writing a book is a big deal, right? But then, as always, reality came crashing down, and I realised that my book still needed some serious work. And by serious work, I mean I had no knowledge of the publishing process and needed someone else to help me cross the finish line. Enter Master Mike Swope, the man I contacted when I reached a point where I couldn't continue on my own.

Now, let me just say, Mike is a pretty cool dude. We met through The Study of Taekwondo group on Facebook a few years ago, and we've been online buddies ever since. We're both into martial arts, movies, and sharing life experiences, so it was a huge honour when he invited me to write a recommendation for his grandmaster's book, Taekwon-Do: Origins of the Art: Bok Man Kim's Historical Photospective (1955 – 2015). And to top it off, he even interviewed me for a cover story on Totally Tae Kwon Do magazine.

I was hoping to just hand off the project to Mike, but he had other ideas. When I submitted the manuscript, I thought I was done with the hard work of writing. But Mike's initial feedback was to consider re-writing the manuscript using my voice and telling my story. This would elevate the project and make it more interesting for the reader. Now, I'm not one to argue with an expert, so I began contemplating an overhaul of the manuscript, even though I felt like there was no gas left in the tank.

But that was just the beginning of the process. We edited the book, not just for layout and flow, but for grammar and punctuation, blurred and missing pictures, and to ensure the accuracy of headers and sub-headers. And we did all of this right up until the final upload for the printer, two years after working together on the project.

Now, here's where things get interesting. Mike needed to understand many concepts through the chapters, which were foreign to him and probably readers as well. The JDK training method seeks same-side and opposite-side solutions for every tactic wherever possible. Additionally, we have less reservations than other schools when reaching for either hard-style and soft-style solutions as we deep dive into traditional techniques.

Master Mike Swope, Author Master Colin Wee, Will Just, and Jeff Palm

As martial arts literature goes, little of what we needed to present is what you'd expect in a regular instructional manual. In the hard style "One Hit-One Kill" world view, many practitioners are taught to believe each technique comes with a guarantee of success. To assume the possibility of failure, to invite non-compliance from the opponent, to introduce workarounds, and then to share the recipe for this "secret sauce" is simply unprecedented, to our knowledge. We believe this makes Breaking Through unique and valuable in the field of martial arts books.

But let's be real here: it's not always a smooth sailing journey when it comes to writing. Mike believed we could create a book that was the next best thing to sliced bread. He went above and beyond to ensure my writing was in line with my beliefs. I was happy to jump into that rabbit hole with him. I was happy being brought to the edge of my ability. This has to be part of the journey too, right?

It was difficult enough trying to make progress despite facing challenges from a global pandemic, time zones differences between author and publisher, and the goal to represent 3-dimensional concepts on 2-dimensional pages. A minor stumbling block was the various photo shoots we had to organise to represent the material in the book.

We had done the first photo shoot with the initial draft of the manuscript in 2019, but two years later we needed additional photos for expanded explanations and re-takes on some of the originals. And we booked yet another photo session at the end of 2022 to redo some photos.

Eventually we found ourselves some ways into the first quarter of 2023, feeling the time pressure from the release date of March 23, 2023 at the American Karate and Taekwondo Organization Annual Seminars in Dallas, Texas. We still had final edits to make, e-proofs to closely review, and pre-order web pages to set up. Plus, I had been invited to teach several sessions for the event, as well as several seminars at various schools near and around Dallas.

I was excited about the AKATO event but had trouble getting time to develop my teaching plan until I was done with the book. The seven sessions I would teach, I decided, would present combative insights from various Karate and Taekwondo combative forms, and how they can be applied in specific scenarios. I intended to share with seminar attendees JDK's insights, our journey of discovery, snippets from Breaking Through, and a good dose of humour which included several dad jokes.

As I shared news of the seminar and book launch road trip on social media, two black belts associated with me and JDK online were so inspired that they scheduled flights to join us in Dallas.

The first black belt, Jeff Palm, trained with my school in Australia 10 years ago and found our practice complementary to his own training. And the second black belt, Will Just, found my blog 5 years ago, has been in contact with me through email since, and in a leap of faith, came to Dallas to be my seminar partner.

> About: Colin Wee is the Principal of Joong Do Kwan in Perth Western Australia. Colin has recently published a book titled Breaking Through: The Secrets of Bassai Dai Kata. He has practiced three systems in three countries for four decades. Formerly an Assistant National Coach in Archery, Colin is now known as a traditional applications specialist amongst his friends.

Now, my school is not about inflicting pain and suffering. But there is something to be said for feeling traditional tactics firsthand. I admit that Will, as my seminar partner, was practically tortured during our training sessions. But he didn't complain, smiled through the discomfort, and made huge strides in understanding as he experienced receiving traditional concepts first-hand. This is the empirical knowledge he needed, making him a better all-round practitioner.

The road trippers, once shown our practice, came to be extremely helpful to other seminar participants. Moving between roles as demonstration partners to assisting with the participants, they were an unexpected blessing to help me communicate concepts and techniques.

Around 170-180 martial arts practitioners attended those seven seminars in and around Dallas. I expect the enthusiasm they displayed, the positive feedback to the material presented, and the buzz of energy I felt throughout the sessions will feed my very soul for many years to come.

I wrote Breaking Through: The Secrets of Bassai Dai Kata because I wanted to express my gratitude for my teachers and share my unique insight after 40 years in martial arts. To be absolutely honest, I have felt self-conscious as people ask for autographs and praise the book. I mean, it's not like I'm some sort of celebrity. I'm just a humble martial artist who knew to reach out to a team of people to help me get several things off my chest.

All joking aside, this whole experience has been amazing. From writing the book to finally holding the finished product, it's been a journey I'll never forget. And who knows, maybe I'll write another book someday. [Someone please stop me!]

Frequently asked questions

Why should my community group or organisation sign up for Containers for Change?

Because it's an awesome way to rally your community together and raise funds while helping the environment! Not to mention the sense of achievement when your team smashes its goals and is able to purchase new sporting or playground equipment for your club; provide funds for vital community groups; or help enrich the lives of others through worthwhile causes. With over $1.4 million dollars already been raised by WA causes, every container brings endless possibilities!

Why do we need Containers for Change?

It is estimated that more than 500 million eligible 10¢ containers end up as litter or in landfill every year, even though the materials they are made from can be recycled into a range of things – including new containers. By providing a 10¢ refund, we're giving everyone an incentive to keep containers out of landfill and give them another life. Containers for Change also supports community groups, charities and provides job opportunities for West Australians.

What can I return?

Think of drink containers that are more likely to be consumed on the go, as the ones that can be returned for a refund - water, soft drinks, fruit juice drinks, flavoured milk and single serve alcoholic containers are all included. Containers that are not included are white milk, wine bottles, pure spirit bottles, food cans and anything over 3 litres. This is because most of us are already doing a great job of recycling these at home. The 10¢ icon found on most containers is an easy way to see if it is eligible. But if you're not sure, scan the barcode using the Containers for Change app and it will instantly tell you if it's a 10¢ container. The Containers for Change website also gives a quick and clear rundown of what's in and what's out.

What is a member number?

A Member Number is your unique code that you receive once you sign up to Containers for Change. When you take your containers to a refund point, you simply provide your member number and the funds are immediately transferred to your nominated bank account. How easy is that! You can also invite anyone to donate their container funds to your organisation by entering your Member Number at any refund point.

What is a refund point and how to I find one near me?

Refund points will sort and count your containers and process your refunds. There are more than 200 refund point locations across Western Australia, which are listed on the Containers for Change website. Some refund points can also provide your group with donation bins and bags.

Visit **containersforchange.com.au/wa** to find out more.

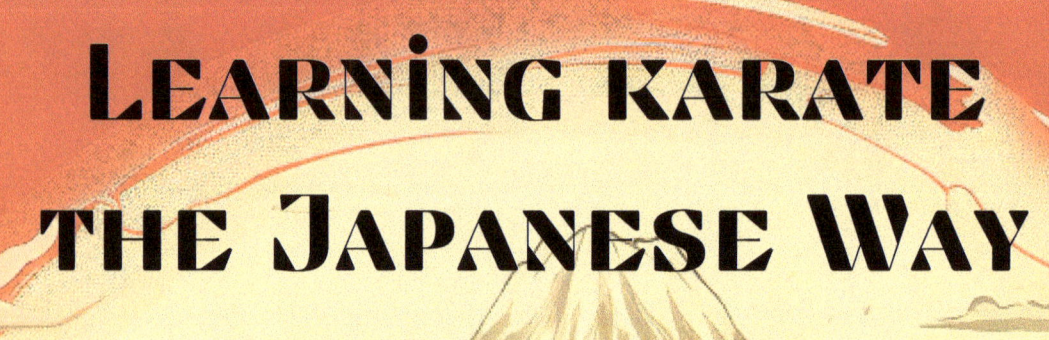

Learning Karate the Japanese Way

by
Mike Clarke Kyoshi 8th dan

"True karate is this: that in daily life one's mind and body be trained in the spirit of humility; and that in critical times one be devoted utterly to the cause of justice."
Funakoshi Gichin

In the words of the man all Shotokan karateka, regardless of affiliation, look to as their founding father (their model), there is no mention of 'true' karate being competitive. Nor do his words point to the need to be better than anyone else. His words offer advice to the individual, because karate can only exist in the heart and mind of the individual. Irrespective of how large the group, or how legendary the leader, karate itself remains unconstrained by group ego and tribal thinking. Regardless of the cognitive duality some are happy to accommodate, you simply can't have 'alternative' truths. Why? Because a variety of truths lead to friction, turmoil, and eventually to hell. Here is a basic truth that's conveniently ignored by many Shotokan karateka, Funakoshi Gichin sensei, an Okinawan, never practiced or taught Japanese Shotokan. His karate was Okinawan Shorin-ryu.

In the goldfish bowl that most karateka live out their existence, it is easy to accept the all-knowing knowledge of their leader and seniors. Yet, it takes very little to dispel the illusion. The justice Funakoshi sensei spoke of relies on 'real' truth, not the 'alternative' kind proving so popular these days. For many karateka, the stories they learn growing up are remarkably similar. Often, only the names and locations change, the result of a good story's common appeal. In one group, the legendary figure fought a bull, in another, he defeats a notorious boxer. The details change, but the myth remains the same, told and retold to underscore in the initiate's mind just how 'righteous' the group is. And so, the blurring of truth and myth begins.

Looking back to justify the present is an exercise fraught with danger, yet it's a very common practice. Religions do it, politicians do it, and karate people do it too. It is an exercise where facts don't really matter, and the truth is marginalised in favour of a convenient view of things based solely on the current agenda of the group. With karate, it is not always possible to know 'now' exactly what occurred back 'then'. Sometimes, it's impossible to even pinpoint when 'then' was. Karate's true value however has always been found in 'now'. Right now, is yesterday's future. Right now, is tomorrow's past; there has only ever been 'right now'. With thirty-three years' experience interviewing karate 'leaders' from around the planet, and fifty-years of training behind me, I believe I can speak a little to the common threads that run through today's karate world. You may not be aware such strands exist. In fact, I can guarantee you know nothing of them unless you've spent a reasonable amount of time outside your own particular goldfish bowl. For a significant number of readers, your first glimpse of the familiar outside of your group may come as a shock. If that's the case, I hope it's a shock you'll never recover from.

The foundation story.
Every group, style, and association teaching a Japanese martial art today has its own foundation story. Each of them contains a kernel of truth, but that's usually as far as it goes. The story's role is not to provide the truth, its role is to create an impression in the initiate's mind.

An impression that sets you and your tribe apart from others. Soon after joining the group, and almost invisibly, your sense of 'self' slips away unnoticed. No longer seeing yourself for who you are and what you stand for, you begin to validate yourself more by who you are not. You are not like those idiots in that other group/style/martial art, you don't do things like them, you don't do your kata that way, your group doesn't give grades away, the list is endless. When thoughts like these enter your mind, the seed of group thinking sown on day one has germinated, producing yet another crop of compliant individuals ready for harvest. And let's be clear, the turnover of students is so large in the world of commercial karate these days, a new harvest is needed every few months just to keep the teacher employed. Hence the fertiliser thrown around by those who would farm your desire to learn karate for their own financial/egotistical interest. First lesson free, regular gradings, family friendly fun, and perhaps the biggest single piece of bull sh*t to be offered to the initiate: recognition.

It may surprise some of you reading this, but not all, that karate is not and never has been held in high regard in Japan. It's standing within the pantheon of traditional martial arts is low. Hardly surprising when you consider karate's shambolic beginnings in that country just a century ago, and later, the squalid arguments over succession that erupt with depressing regularity following the death of a significant leader. You may be familiar with the lengthy legal battle fought by rival factions within the JKA some years ago, but that event was not unique. The same thing happened within the Kyokushinkai following the death of its founder, Mas Oyama. Shito-ryu, Wado-ryu, and Goju-ryu too, have all witnessed a similar process. Budo principles being swept away by greed and avarice, how very uninspiring.

I have long been unsure why any self-respecting karateka outside of Japan feels a need to be recognised by karateka who happen to live there. Alfa-males, and other inadequate personalities to one side, I wonder how a very small number of Japanese karateka knowing your name is going to make any difference at all to who 'you' are?

The path well-travelled.
There are two main streams of thought prevalent in karate these days. The first looks to Japan/Okinawa for leadership and guidance. The second doesn't. Ironically, it hardly matters which side of the divide you stand, as very few groups passing on karate today have abandoned the 'Seven steps of learning' so long ingrained in Japanese culture. You may not have heard of these 'steps' before now, but I can guarantee your education in karate has been influenced by them. And though I'm not a gambling man, I'm willing to bet a great many of you reading of them here for the first time will find them entirely familiar.

1. Copying the model.
Gaining mastery of the 'model's' technique is paramount. This is done by rigorous instruction followed by 'stealing' techniques via observation and solo practice. Interpretation is strongly discouraged, and creativity is allowed only after a great many years of study.

2. Discipline.

Teachers will stress the necessity of severity to their students. And bring to bear various levels of physical and psychological hardships that must be endured by the student in order to promote in them a sense of personal growth. Above all else, students are encouraged to be loyal and persevere.

3. The master – student relationship.

The roles of sensei and deshi (teacher and student) are clearly defined, becoming a line that must not be crossed. For both parties an image of the founder, the ideal practitioner of their art, exists in their imagination and is considered by both the teacher and student to be 'the model'.

4. Secrets, stages, and the hierarchy of study.

Teachers impart the techniques of the art in hierarchical stages marked by the granting of certificates, ranks, and titles. Progress in the art takes place by memorising an increased repertoire of movements. In many cases, 'advanced' techniques require no more skill to execute than those taught to a beginner. The 'advanced' student being someone who has simply had more time to practice what to do.

5. Established lineages.

In Japan, various organisations and their affiliates exist for every school dedicated to a particular art. Their legitimacy was often established on nothing more than a tenuous link back to the founder. Despite immeasurable physical and moral differences evolving over time, groups, for the sake of authenticity, hold fast to the notion of being linked to a founder (the model).

6. Non-verbal communication.

Teachers often stress non-verbal forms of communication by insisting students simply follow (imitate) the model provided to them by their teacher (example). What oral communication there is often comes in the form of jargon, metaphors, and parables…and sometimes, downright lies.

7. The art as a spiritual quest.

The study of the art is positioned as a gateway to a higher level of spiritual understanding. The ultimate goal no longer mastery of the physical techniques and how to use them, but instead, mastery of the 'self'. Questioning the inconsistencies often observed by students between the teachings of the 'model' (founder) and the 'example' (teacher) standing in front of them is strongly discouraged.

To the Japanese way of thinking then, the 'way' of karate appears to be no more special a path through life than the 'way' of any other artistic pursuit. Here's something to think about…what you draw from your experience studying karate depends entirely on what you bring with you when you begin, and what you do when you encounter problems along the way. As far as I'm aware, change is the only constant in the universe. You might say, "What about energy?" Well, you're right. But consider for a moment that without the ability to change form, energy too would stop. With this example, I wonder sometimes if nature isn't whispering to us that change, rather than a corrupted notion of tradition is, if considered, a fundamental necessity to experiencing not only growth but a balanced way of life. The longer you live and the longer you practice karate, the more important it becomes to understand the lesson here. Stick to what you've always done, and you'll always be what you always were: stuck! Therefore, traditional karateka have to ask themselves… 'What exactly is the tradition I'm claiming to propagate?'

Making gods of men.

It is not uncommon to come across this phenomenon in the karate world, especially if the 'god' in question is no longer alive. And even when they are still breathing, a great many karateka place their teachers on pedestals so high it's a wonder they don't suffer permanent nose bleeds. There is a word for it, it's called 'Apotheosis'. I have met several 'karate gods' over the years. The best of them were sublimely human. But a few had serious, and obvious, phycological problems as a result of believing their own publicity. Not only is it unhealthy to 'give' yourself over to another person, it is also downright dangerous to your financial security and mental wellbeing. When you begin to see something 'other worldly' in another human being, it's time to take a long, hard look at yourself. The need for heroes has always been an easy path to exploitation, and nowhere more so than in the esoteric world of martial arts. And while it is often beneficial to your own growth to take inspiration from the growth in others, there is no need to lose perspective. You should never make gods of men. No one you'll ever meet in a gi is anything other than a human being. Remember that the next time you suspend your 'common-sense'. Remember, it too when the gap between what they say and what they do fails to reflect your own understanding of self-improvement.

Most of the (said to be 50 million plus) karateka in the world are not Japanese. Nor are they Okinawan. The overwhelming majority of people who identify as karateka today come from countries and cultures far removed from Yamoto*. Strange then, that an archaic and idiosyncratic Japanese way of learning continues to prevail.

Okinawan karate teachers have long ignored their Japanese neighbours when it comes to the 'way' of karate, but in doing so they have paid a heavy price. Ridiculed, bullied, and treated disgracefully by karate's political elite in Japan. Okinawan sensei today live in a kind of karate no-man's-land. And while it's true to say that many karate sensei on the island do their best to maintain their traditional ways, a great many have surrendered over time to the stick and carrot approach adopted by Japan. Tokyo's begrudging acceptance that Okinawa, and not Japan, is the physical and spiritual home of karate, was paid for by denying Okinawa any role in the recent Olympic games where, as many of you know, a form of karate exhibitionism was introduced.

As well, the promised amount of funding to establish a purpose-built training facility on Okinawa to showcase karate and kobudo, the Karatedo Kaikan, never materialised. The complex of buildings seen today is barely half the size of the original concept planned for the Kaikan. Okinawa, once an island paradise with a vibrant and unique culture that gave birth to karate, continues to pay the price for the rigidity of Japanese thinking and their unambiguous self-righteousness. Screaming American jets that fly low overhead, and the constant landing and take-off of heavy military aircraft over built up areas, has made life for many Okinawans a living hell. The accidents, the crime, the rapes, and the refusal of the Japanese government to do anything other than appease their American allies, continues to reflect the true relationship between Japan and Okinawa as one of master and subordinate, parent and child.

The key characteristics of iemoto seido are no doubt recognisable to all karateka with more than a couple of years training behind them. The emphasis on the master-pupil relationship, the established hierarchical order within the 'family/group', the unquestioning authority of the head, the 'iemoto/head of the house'. The underlying sense within the group of exclusivity as far as being authentic, traditional, and being right! Those who have made a detailed study of Japanese culture sometimes refer to iemoto seido as 'closing the circle' and think of it in terms of providing the model for how Japanese institutions, indeed Japanese society as a whole, conduct themselves. Schools, companies, political parties, even the yakuza*, in fact any group in Japan large or small, exhibit similar traits and conduct themselves in ways easily recognisable as stemming from the notion of iemoto seido.

But you shouldn't be surprised to learn this, right? After all, Japanese karate is just another sub-culture, and was never likely to be organised in any other way before being introduced to the rest of the world. Their view of karate, unlike the art in its native Okinawa, was never going to allow for individualism, either in thought or movement. If you're a nail determined to stand up, you will be hammered back down, because that's the Japanese way. Offend the 'family' and suffer the consequences.

There is an aside to the iemoto seido system that like its physical counterpart, is easily recognisable to karateka today. Whereas iemoto seido is a structure, a skeleton if you like upon which an activity can be hung, the actual art, or skill (techniques), is known as 'ieryu' or 'house style'. To the Japanese mind it is not enough to be good at the art you practise, or to have developed a deep understanding of it, you have to be 'recognised' by others. The greater the recognition, the greater your standing (sounds familiar, right?).

Okay, so here is the truth of it. Back when the Tokugawa shogunate (ruling elite) were slipping away, it identified in certain artistic endeavours a means by which specific nobles might create a source of income for themselves. So, the shogunate assigned these families exclusive rights to receive payment for certifying the non-noble practitioners of various arts. This idea of 'recognition' remains a powerful selling point in many arts to this day, including karate. But in truth it is little more than a 'arubaito', a cash-in-hand side job that brings in extra income. In Japan today there are any number of 'iemoto' (head of the house) presiding over any number of 'ryu' (schools). From dance, acting, flower arranging, and even how to slice live fish before serving, there are iemoto ready and willing to 'recognise' you as a master of the art…for a price.

As you might expect given the human condition, money, and not skill, is often at the heart of keeping these 'traditional' ryu/schools alive. Thousands of dollars change hands each year between those wanting to be recognised, and those who by happy chance find themselves with the appropriate certificate and stamp to fulfill their need. Accordingly, an illusion of progress is established. However, inferior skills are often authenticated and individuals with suspect characters regularly gain promotion. And for both, outrageous fees are charged to move from one rank to the next. But it's not only when people are 'on the make' that the iemoto seido system proves problematic in an educational sense. When an individual behaves contrary to the view or wishes of the iemoto, they are divorced from the entire group. Ostracised by everyone for fear of being punished in similar fashion. Group consciousness is required to maintain the iemoto's control, the exclusiveness, and the sense of 'us' and 'them'. Individuals who disturb the façade, and other groups within the same discipline are therefore viewed as rivals, to be considered as opponents and treated accordingly.

The karate found in Japan is in many ways little different from that found in other countries. More intense in many cases for sure, but still locked into a familiar rigidity of thought and appreciation for karate you can find anywhere around the world. Hardly surprising when you consider how hard various Japanese karate schools worked to spread their particular version of the art internationally. How much of karate's teachings have been lost or replaced during its global migration from Japan is evident in today's infantile attempt to resurrect 'oyo' under the confused banner of 'bunkai'.

I shake my head watching their efforts… karateka with answers desperately searching for the right questions. You simply can't orchestrate a fight, not a real one anyway. I have read the phrase, 'principle before technique' many times in various publications over the years and wondered why so few karateka have actually adopted the idea. Understanding iemoto seido is the closest I have come to an answer.

In recent times, it has become acceptable to adhere to 'alternative' truths by basing your opinions on 'alternative' facts. "Everyone's entitled to their own opinion," isn't that the standard logic applied these days? While the latter might be true, it's not the same thing as having the right to express your opinion. That particular 'right', as with all other rights, comes at a cost. The price for articulating your opinion is paid for, in advance, with experience. It's a simple idea really, if you haven't paid to acquire it then an opinion isn't yours to express. And if that's the case, then you might at least have the maturity and good manners to keep your opinion to yourself. According to the iemoto seido model, my thoughts on karate expressed in this article will be thrown away as quickly as possible. Not because they are unworthy of further consideration, but because I'm an outsider as far as your particular group is concerned. How easy then, according to the education many of you have received so far, to dismiss everything you've just read and move on.

As Michelangelo wrote long, long, ago….
"The problem with man is not that he aims too high, and misses; but that he aims to low and hits."
My thinking is this…the quest for all martial artists should be to prove him wrong.

*Yamoto – The ancient name for Japan.
** Yakuza – Organized criminal gangs similar to the Italian Mafia.

References:
Transmitting tradition by the rules: Robert J Smith
Seven characteristics of a traditional approach to learning: Gary De Coker

Books by Michael Clarke
Available where all good books are sold!

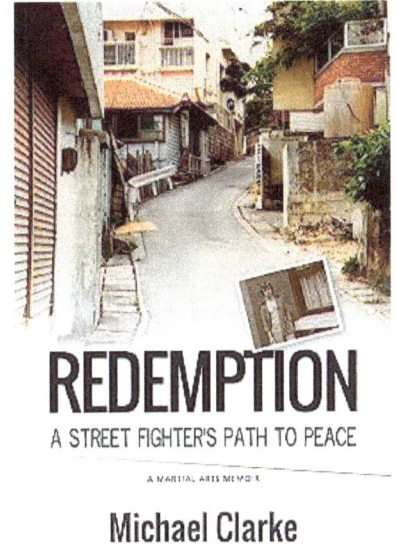

Michael Clarke, Kyoshi 8th dan, has practiced karate since 1974 and Kobudo since 2006. He has authored more than five hundred articles and six books and is renowned worldwide for his honesty and insight.

Maintaining Motivation When Training Alone

by
Sensei Natasha Fabian 4th Dan

I have been practicing Shukokai Karate Do since 1997. My journey began in a town called Wickham, where I trained for 3 years until my Sensei left the town. I took over the running of the club at the age of 17 with the support of the WA Chief Instructor who is based in Carnarvon (700 kms or 8 hrs drive away). In 2006, I relocated to Perth and took a FIFO position, all the while continuing to train, teach, and grade. I worked FIFO on and off for about 10 years, during this time my nearest Senior Instructors were in Carnarvon or Melbourne.

I have spent about 50% of my karate journey training remotely by myself and I would like to share my experiences and insights in hopes that it may help you in yours. I think this topic is even more relevant considering how COVID has impacted the martial arts community over the past three years and there is still some uncertainty surrounding the future. So without further ado here are my tips for maintaining motivation when training alone:

Understand what motivates you – Are you intrinsically or extrinsically motivated? To find out more visit:

https://betterup.com/blog/types-of-motivation

Then ask yourself:

- *How much do I want it?*
- *What will I gain?*
- *What am I willing to invest in or sacrifice to achieve the outcome?*

Be intentional with your training – Set up a monthly routine incorporating mini goals and reward yourself when you achieve them (e.g., tell a friend or family member, treat yourself with something small – I like to use a food reward on my cheat day). Remember, your goals need to be SMART – Specific, Measurable, Achievable, Realistic, Time Based. Above all, make your training fun, vary it and don't be afraid to get creative.

Make yourself accountable – You can do this in a number of ways. Join forces with another solo trainer and periodically share your training progress. Help each other stay motivated. Similarly, you could do the same thing with a mentor, meet once a month (phone / video call / in person) to discuss your progress. If both of those aren't an option, then think about keeping a training journal/diary/video log.

Review your progress and readjust – If you are keeping a training journal/diary, then this is a little easier. Another great tool I found was to film myself, then self-critique it. When reviewing yourself, think about whether you have achieved your short-term goals. Check whether those goals are still aligned with the main goal. Remember, sometimes we may have to make minor adjustments or change our course entirely (don't be afraid to do the latter). Plan for setbacks in your training (e.g. injury, illness, personal drama) and have a strategy. For example, when I get injured I either modify my training around the injury or if that isn't possible, I practice visualisation and review my karate video library.

I still use these techniques today, even as a 4th Dan preparing for the next goal. Currently, I train/teach once a month via video with the other WA Shukokai Instructors, to focus on our development, both as students and instructors. The International Shukokai Instructors (3rd Dan and above) also gather via video once a month to work on the more advanced aspects of self-defence. Technology has made it easier than ever to stay connected and it has re-ignited my enthusiasm for my training. I hope this article helps you with yours.

Sensei Natasha Fabian
4th Dan, Instructor,
Samurai Karate Belmont
Enquires: 0417 939 037 or
Samurai Karate Belmont Facebook

The acronym SMART stands for Specific, Measurable, Achievable, Relevant, and Time-bound. Each of these elements is essential in setting goals that are both effective and attainable. Specific goals are clear and well-defined. They should be focused on a particular aspect of training, such as improving a specific technique or increasing strength. Measurable goals are those that can be quantified so that progress can be tracked and evaluated. This can be accomplished by setting benchmarks or milestones that can be used to determine how successful a particular goal has been.

A goal should be achievable, meaning it is realistic and attainable with the resources available. Relevant goals are those that are directly tied to your overall training plan and align with your long-term objectives. Finally, goals should be time bound, meaning they should have a specific deadline for completion.

To apply SMART goals to training, it is important to identify areas that need improvement and set specific goals to address those areas. For example, you may want to improve your striking technique and set a goal to land 100 punches on a heavy bag in a single training session. This goal is specific, measurable, achievable, relevant, and time bound.

Once a SMART goal has been set, it is important to create a plan of action to achieve it. This might involve breaking the goal down into smaller, more manageable steps, or identifying the resources and support needed to accomplish the goal. Regularly monitoring progress is also key to successful goal setting. By tracking progress and evaluating results, you can adjust your approach as needed to stay on track and achieve your desired outcomes.

SMART goals can help you focus your efforts, track progress, and achieve your objectives. By setting specific, measurable, achievable, relevant, and time-bound goals, you can establish a clear path to success and continue to improve your skills over time.
Check out our SMART worksheets - ED

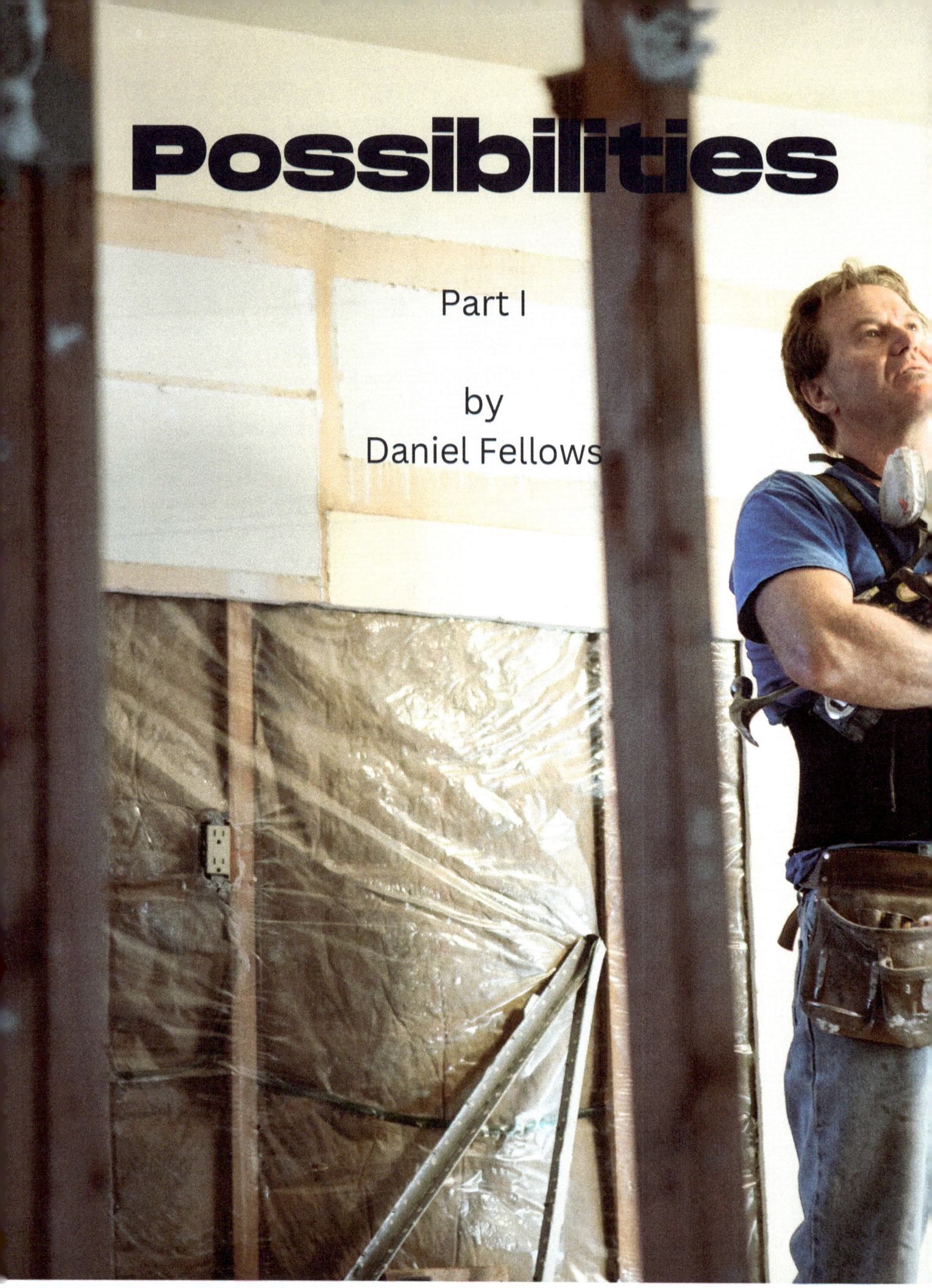

Possibilities

Part I

by
Daniel Fellows

The heavy chain clinked and rattled as Brian tried the key in the padlock. The real estate agent had given him the right one, the key matched the lock perfectly. It had inserted, and the barrel was turning slightly, just not enough for the shackle to release. He didn't want to force the key too much, it could snap and add another problem to an already long list of dilemmas he was facing.

"Twist damn you," he muttered.

He jiggled the key again. It turned, and the shackle sprang open, causing the heavy chain to fall loose, landing in a coiled heap at his feet like a heavy, dead snake. He pushed open the door, and the hinges groaned under the weight of the heavy double doors.

Brian had driven past the shop front on more than a few occasions. From the street, he could tell the place was run down and needed dire repairs; a new front window, fresh paint and some kind of decorative design that would scream for new clients to come and visit the new dojo in town. The front didn't need too much work. The inside of the store was a completely different story. He could see the possibilities, but could his daughter Kaylee?

"Oh. My. God," Kaylee said.

"I know," Brian said. "Isn't it beautiful?"

"Beautiful? If by beautiful you mean the third site where the Americans dropped a nuclear bomb… Hiroshima, Nagasaki and this place. How has this site not been condemned and torn down?"

"Oh. come on. It's not that bad. Look at the size of this place. It's perfect." He spun around, taking in the entire shop interior. His expression was that of a father seeing his newborn for the first time.

"What about that gaping hole in the floorboards over there?" she pointed. "Or the graffiti? Which I assume was written by primary school kids or illiterate adults because of the spelling… and the water damage over there in the corner. And that's just what I can see." She walked around the perimeter of the floor space, her head shaking.

Brian's expression didn't change despite Kaylee pointing out the obvious flaws the shop presented. It was like he was a little kid in a candy shop, minus the candy and with a lot more dust and debris.

"I don't think you are seeing what I am seeing," he said.

She walked around pallets of disused equipment and rusty tools left by workmen who had been doing who knows what possibly years ago. Packets of empty cement littered the floor and piles of mouldy, discarded food had attracted flies and cockroaches. "I am a hard pass on this one, dad," Kaylee said, walking toward the door.

"Don't you hear it?" he asked. He cupped a hand over his ear and cocked his head, listening to something only he could hear.

"The only thing I can hear is the sound of money being poured down a drain."

"It's the sound of over a hundred students, from white belt to black shouting kiai in shiko dachi while punching chudan tsuki."

Kaylee cupped her own hand to hear for a second and then shook her head. "Nope. Still money going down a drain."

"And on that wall, there will be a mirror so the students can watch themselves in their karate gis. On this wall will be student of the month portraits, and further along will be nunchakus and tonfas for when we have weapons night." He walked along the wall, holding up his hands indicating where each item would go.

"And mats on the floor, I suppose?" Kaylee asked, visualising what her dad was describing.

"Nope. Floorboards or nothing. And over here on the door would be posters of the principles of karate and dojo etiquette."

"There must be another venue that would be more suited to your first dojo in the area, dad," Kaylee pleaded with him.

"We've both looked, and we both know this is the one. The size, the location, parking. The possibilities. This venue has a lot of potential. Or should I say, this dojo."

She tried again. She looked at the mess, the debris and the damage and could see a dojo full of students wearing the same karate gi's with her dad's hand drawn logo. Students from wall to wall in varying grades. Her dad out front leading in kata or combination.

"This area needs this, Kaylee," he said. "We need this."

She dropped into shiko dachi and threw a punch. Her kiai echoed off the walls and reverberated around the room.

"That's my girl," Brian said.

As Kaylee stepped from the venue, Brian looked back and glanced around the room. He saw the backs of his students performing their katas and combinations and kumite, and the possibilities of this building never seemed more positive.

Part II in the next edition of MAWA.

Daniel Fellows is an author living and working in Perth, Western Australia. When he isn't writing and spending time with his wife and five children, he is driving dump trucks on an iron ore mine site in the Pilbara region of Western Australia. Daniel has a wide range of interests including: Karate, playing bass guitar, learning German and reading history books.

Daniel's books are available where all good books are sold.

BE YOUR BEST WITH GOOD SPORTS

About the Good Sports program
The Good Sports program supports and inspires community sporting clubs to set up a better environment for players, volunteers, supporters and officials, helping tackle tricky topics such as alcohol, drugs, smoking, mental health and safe transport.
It involves over 11,000 Australian clubs across more than 100 sporting codes, reaching millions of people. The Alcohol and Drug Foundation has been running the program for two decades.
Becoming a Good Sports club sends an important message to club members and the community.
It confirms that your club promotes a responsible attitude towards alcohol and smoking, supports members' mental health and safety on the roads, and provides a safer and more welcoming environment for players, members, families and supporters.

The results speak for themselves. Studies show that Good Sports clubs experience a:
- 42% in alcohol-related incidents
- 37% decrease in risky drinking.

Why it matters
Local sporting clubs look after their members' wellbeing, both on and off the field.
Good Sports provides support to clubs on issues such as mental health, alcohol management, smoking, illegal drugs and safe transport.
For over 20 years, the program has worked with a variety of clubs; from those with a liquor license, those where alcohol is only consumed occasionally, to clubs that are completely alcohol and smoke-free.

Benefits for clubs
- Even if you don't sell alcohol or have BYO events, you'll be able to set standards around smoking and drug risk management to build a positive culture.
- Helps clubs develop a strong governance framework. Good Sports take the guesswork out of understanding and complying with legal requirements, such as smoking, alcohol and drug risk management.
- Access to resources and training such as forums, webinars, RSA courses and more.
- Good Sports helps clubs create a safer, more family friendly environment, helping to attract even more families, members and volunteers.
- Good Sports gives you tips, resources and inspiration from other successful clubs to help you explore new funding opportunities.
- Clubs with a positive community profile and reputation can jump to the front when it comes to securing local sponsorships.
- Good Sports helps you attract and keep volunteers. Clubs that progress through the program using the handy volunteer tool kits and resources can save hours of admin time.

Benefits to communities

- Members, families and guests are more connected and satisfied with their community.
- Can help to reduce violence, noise, injury and damage to facilities.
- Can help to reduce road trauma and drink-driving incidents.
- There's an increased level of responsibility taken by sports clubs for member behaviour.
- Clubs have greater legal compliance, stronger governance and increased awareness in addressing alcohol-related issues.
- More young people are educated about mental health, alcohol and other drugs.
- Improved health and fitness of community members.

How does the program work?

When you sign up to Good Sports you'll become a member of a much larger team, with over 11,000 clubs from more than 100 sporting codes working together to create a winning community sporting club culture.

Community sporting clubs told Good Sports what they need most and the program delivers just that:

- Connection to a dedicated Good Sports team member to step club volunteers through the online program.
- Help to comply with legislation and duty of care requirements.
- Quick and easy access to proven tools and resources.
- Tips to boost funding opportunities.
- Help for busy volunteers to make a positive difference, in less time and with less stress.

And best of all, there's no cost to join Good Sports – it's free for all community sporting clubs in Australia.

Signing up is easy, and you'll have a dedicated Good Sports team member to help if you have any questions or need support along the way.

For more information or to register your club
Web: goodsports.com.au
Email: goodsports@adf.org.au
Facebook: facebook.com/goodsportsclubs
Phone: 1300 883 817

Standing Together

What we can do:

- **Promote healthy and respectful relationships** in the workplace, community and in our personal lives, including talking about and demonstrating respect in our own relationships and to our children
- **Speak out and act** against violence or coercion when we see it; be an 'upstander'
- **Support victims** by offering help and alliance
- **Advocate for policy and social changes** that promote awareness and gender equality

Need Help?

- **Women's Domestic Violence Helpline** - free call 1800 007 339
- **Men's Domestic Violence Helpline** - free call 1800 000 599
- **National Family and Domestic Violence Counselling Service** - 1800 Respect /1800 737 732
- **No to Violence Men's Referral Service** - 133 766 491

For more information contact

Emily

0491 175 880

   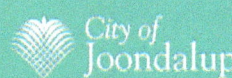 

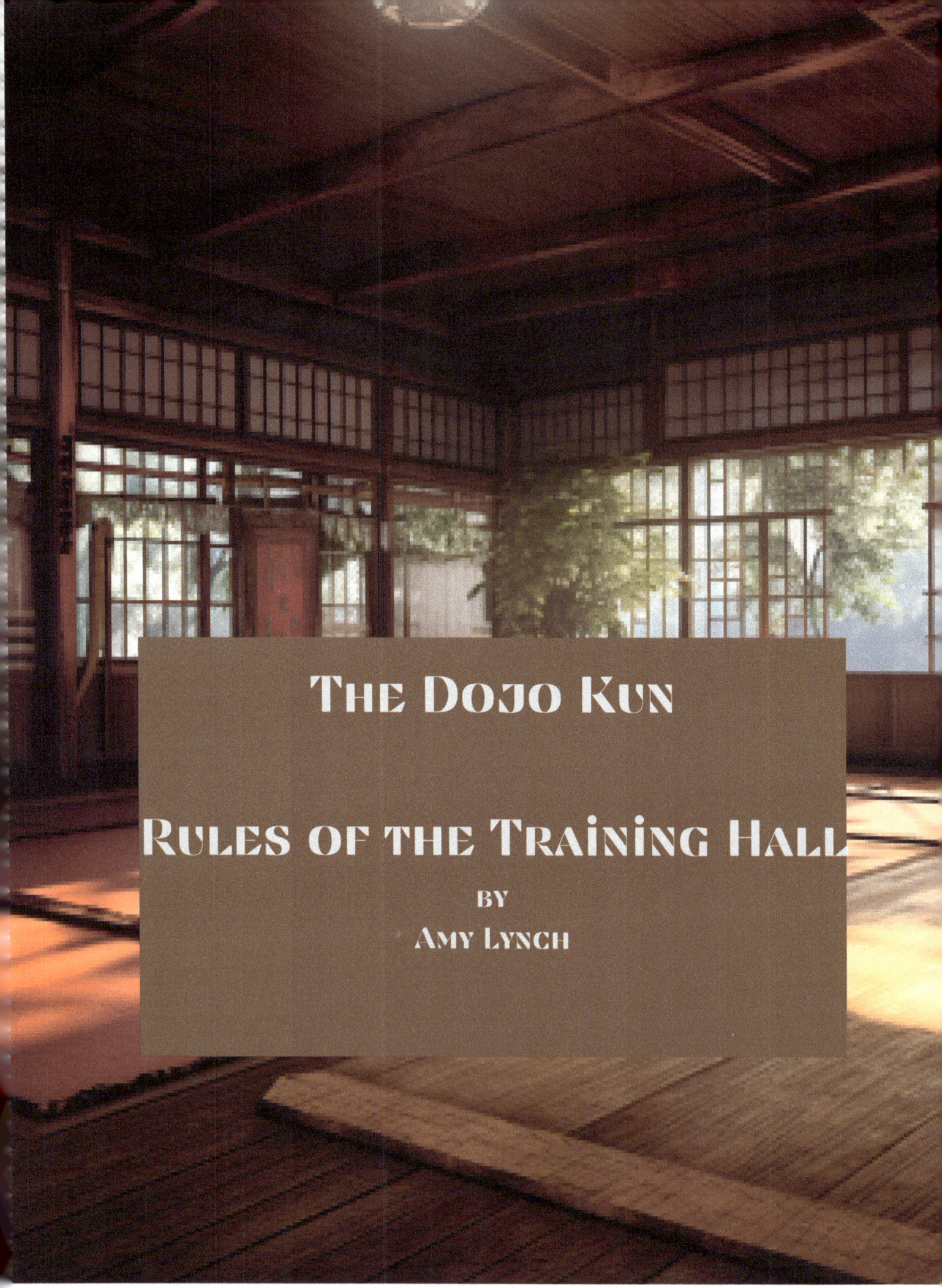

The Dojo Kun

Rules of the Training Hall

By
Amy Lynch

The first known version of the Dojo Kun dates back to the early 1600s, during the Edo period in Japan. It was created by the famous samurai and martial artist Miyamoto Musashi, who wrote "The Book of Five Rings," a treatise on strategy and martial arts. Musashi's Dojo Kun consisted of five principles: "Politeness," "Integrity," "Strength," "Control," and "Perseverance."

Over the years, the Dojo Kun has evolved and been adapted by different martial arts schools and styles. Today, it is commonly recited at the beginning and end of each training session to remind practitioners of the principles that they should strive to embody both on and off the tatami.

In addition to establishing a code of conduct, the Dojo Kun also serves to unify and bond members of the dojo. It provides a shared philosophy and set of values that everyone can work towards, regardless of their skill level or experience.

One of the most famous versions of the Dojo Kun is the one used by the Japan Karate Association (JKA). It consists of five principles, which are as follows:

- Seek perfection of character.
- Be faithful.
- Endeavor.
- Respect others.
- Refrain from violent behavior.

Each principle is accompanied by a brief explanation, such as "Seek perfection of character," which is explained as follows: "To put it simply, seek perfection of character is to strive to be the best person you can be."

While the Dojo Kun has its roots in Japanese martial arts, it is now used in dojos all over the world, regardless of the martial arts style practiced. It has become a universal symbol of the values and principles that martial arts practitioners strive to embody in their daily lives.

In the dojo setting, the Dojo Kun is typically recited by the sensei or the highest-ranking member of the dojo, followed by the students repeating it back in unison. This tradition helps to establish a sense of discipline and respect within the dojo, as well as a sense of unity and community amongst its members.

The Dojo Kun is not just a set of rules to be recited, but rather a philosophy to be lived. It challenges martial arts practitioners to be their best selves, to strive for excellence in all aspects of their lives, and to treat others.

In today's fast-paced and often divided world, the Dojo Kun serves as a reminder of the importance of character, integrity, and respect. It is a timeless tradition that will continue to inspire and guide martial arts practitioners for generations to come. The Dojo Kun is a cornerstone of martial arts philosophy, and its origins have been the subject of much debate and discussion over the years. Some believe that the Dojo Kun was inspired by the Bushido code, which was followed by samurai warriors during the feudal era of Japan.

Others believe that the Dojo Kun was influenced by Zen Buddhism, which emphasises the importance of mindfulness, simplicity, and compassion. Still, others believe that the Dojo Kun was simply an innovation of Miyamoto Musashi himself, who sought to create a set of guidelines for his own students to follow.

Regardless of its origins, the Dojo Kun has become an integral part of the martial arts tradition, and its influence has spread far beyond the dojo walls. In fact, many people who have never trained in martial arts are familiar with the principles of the Dojo Kun, as they have become a popular symbol of discipline and respect.

The Dojo Kun is an important tool for self-improvement and personal growth, as it challenges martial arts practitioners to not only improve their physical abilities but also to cultivate their mental and spiritual well-being. By striving to embody the principles of the Dojo Kun, practitioners can become better versions of themselves, both on and off the mat.

For example, the principle of "Seek perfection of character" encourages practitioners to constantly work on improving themselves, both in terms of their martial arts skills and their personal development. This principle emphasises the importance of setting high standards for oneself and striving to meet them, even when it is difficult or uncomfortable.

Similarly, the principle of "Respect others" reminds practitioners to treat everyone with kindness and compassion, regardless of their background or abilities. This principle encourages practitioners to not only respect their fellow martial artists, but also to show respect to all people they encounter in their daily lives.

It is a powerful symbol of the values and principles that martial arts practitioners strive to embody. It is a testament to the transformative power of martial arts, as it challenges individuals to not only improve their physical strength and abilities, but also their mental and spiritual well-being.

Why not check out what your Dojo Kun says about your style. Think about how you can use it to guide your life in a better direction. Remember that no martial art is ever about just kicking and punching. There is so much more to learn about yourself and your place in the world.

With sincerest thanks to our contributors:

Danni McCullough and Lance Spice - Aikido: Mindfulness in Motion
Gyokunen Kan Aikido - www.ommabudo.com

Chris McVay - My Journey in Martial Arts
Port Kennedy Aikido - https://aikidoportkennedy.com/

Sensei Don Godwin - Early Shukokai Training
Shukokai Karrinyup. Phone: 0450 772 846

Sam Sujatna - Tai Chi the Ultimate Exercise
Perth Tai Chi Academy - https://perthtaichi.com.au - Phone: 0415 165 908

Colin Wee - Unveiling Excellence
Australasian Martial Arts Hall of Fame - https://amahof.asn.au/

Ron Bennett and Bob Brown - The Western Australian Kendo Renmei. Kendo, Iaido & Jodo
https://wakr.asn.au

Maria Francis - Taking Care of Hamstrings (retired masseuse)

Iain Humphreys - Why I love my Homes School Class
Kofukan Karate Mandurah, https://karatemandurah.com

Colin Wee - Breaking Through
https://moosulpublishing.com/breaking-through-the-secrets-of-bassai-dai-kata-by-colin-wee/

Containers for Change - Why should your club get involved?
https://www.containersforchange.com.au/wa/

Michael Clarke, Kyoshi 8th Dan - Learning Karate the Japanese Way
https://ymaa.com/publishing/author/michael-clarke

Sensei Natasha Fabian - Maintaining Motivation When Training Alone
Samurai Karate Belmont Phone: 0417 939 037

Daniel Fellow - Possibilities (serial fiction)
Thriller author - https://www.facebook.com/DFellowsAuthor/

Good Sports - Be Your Best with Good Sports
https://goodsports.com.au

Emily Strange - Anglicare WA - Standing Together
Phone: 0491 175 880

Amy Lynch - The Dojo Kun - Rules of the Training Hall

Write for Us

We are looking for Martial Artists of any style to contribute to our upcoming issues.
We want your authentic story, your journey and the reason WHY you love what you do.
Below is a list of suggested topics. It is not exhaustive, so if you have an idea that we haven't come up with yet, drop us a line.

Training tips; technique workshops; style origins; kids in MA; training fuel; style anatomy; family pages; instructor profile; keeping it real; and more...

MAWA is a quarterly magazine that celebrates and inspires a broad community of Martial Artists across the country. Our goal is to support all MA practitioners. Both instructors and students are encouraged to share their personal experiences, triumphs and challenges within the style they love.

We feature interviews, rants, research, photography, projects and editorials that are respectful to all styles and are keeping in line with our magazine's inclusive philosophy.

Just as no two styles of Martial Arts are alike, our writers should have their own unique voice and tell their story from their own perspective. We encourage you to speak your truth.

Don't worry if you feel that your writing is not up to scratch, just tell us your story, your tip or your instruction the best way you can and our in-house editor will do the rest.

Email your submissions to info@mawamag.com (text in .doc) and (photos in JPEG).

Our goal is to keep MAWA for the Martial Artists, not the profiteers. We will remain advertisement free, while endeavouring to produce a top-quality community magazine that we are all proud of. To keep sale costs low, we cannot offer contributors financial compensation for their submission. However, we will allow you to add your club and organisation's contact information or product/service information to the footnote of your article along with your own bio.

NOTHING
IS IMPOSSIBLE

USE OUR BONUS SMART AND WEEKLY CHECK IN SHEETS TO TRACK YOUR GOALS.

MAWAMAG.COM

SMART GOALS

S SPECIFIC

M MEASURABLE

A ACHIEVABLE

R RELEVANT

T TIME BOUND

SMART GOALS

S — SPECIFIC

M — MEASURABLE

A — ACHIEVABLE

R — RELEVANT

T — TIME BOUND

SMART GOALS

S — SPECIFIC

M — MEASURABLE

A — ACHIEVABLE

R — RELEVANT

T — TIME BOUND

SMART GOALS

S — SPECIFIC

M — MEASURABLE

A — ACHIEVABLE

R — RELEVANT

T — TIME BOUND

Weekly check in

DATE _____

TOP 3 THINGS I DID THIS WEEK
- _____
- _____
- _____

MOST REWARDING INTERACTION I HAD THIS WEEK
_____

THIS WEEK I FELT

NEXT WEEK I WANT TO
_____
_____
_____
_____
_____

THINGS I ACCOMPLISHED THIS WEEK
_____

WHAT WAS THE BEST THING ABOUT THE WEEK?
_____

MY RANKING OF THE WEEK

Weekly check in

DATE _____

TOP 3 THINGS I DID THIS WEEK
- _____
- _____
- _____

THIS WEEK I FELT

MOST REWARDING INTERACTION I HAD THIS WEEK _____

NEXT WEEK I WANT TO _____
_____
_____
_____
_____

THINGS I ACCOMPLISHED THIS WEEK

WHAT WAS THE BEST THING ABOUT THE WEEK? _____

MY RANKING OF THE WEEK

Weekly check in

DATE _____

TOP 3 THINGS I DID THIS WEEK
- _____
- _____
- _____

MOST REWARDING INTERACTION I HAD THIS WEEK

THIS WEEK I FELT

NEXT WEEK I WANT TO
_____
_____
_____
_____

THINGS I ACCOMPLISHED THIS WEEK

WHAT WAS THE BEST THING ABOUT THE WEEK?

MY RANKING OF THE WEEK

Weekly check in

DATE _____

TOP 3 THINGS I DID THIS WEEK
- _____
- _____
- _____

THIS WEEK I FELT

NEXT WEEK I WANT TO
_____
_____
_____
_____

THINGS I ACCOMPLISHED THIS WEEK

MOST REWARDING INTERACTION I HAD THIS WEEK

WHAT WAS THE BEST THING ABOUT THE WEEK?

MY RANKING OF THE WEEK

Weekly check in

DATE _____

TOP 3 THINGS I DID THIS WEEK
- _____
- _____
- _____

MOST REWARDING INTERACTION I HAD THIS WEEK

THIS WEEK I FELT

NEXT WEEK I WANT TO
_____
_____
_____
_____

THINGS I ACCOMPLISHED THIS WEEK

WHAT WAS THE BEST THING ABOUT THE WEEK?

MY RANKING OF THE WEEK

Weekly check in

DATE _____

TOP 3 THINGS I DID THIS WEEK
- _____
- _____
- _____

MOST REWARDING INTERACTION I HAD THIS WEEK _____

THIS WEEK I FELT

NEXT WEEK I WANT TO _____

_____
_____
_____
_____

THINGS I ACCOMPLISHED THIS WEEK

WHAT WAS THE BEST THING ABOUT THE WEEK?

MY RANKING OF THE WEEK

Weekly check in

DATE _____

TOP 3 THINGS I DID THIS WEEK
- _____
- _____
- _____

THIS WEEK I FELT

NEXT WEEK I WANT TO
_____
_____
_____
_____

THINGS I ACCOMPLISHED THIS WEEK

MOST REWARDING INTERACTION I HAD THIS WEEK

WHAT WAS THE BEST THING ABOUT THE WEEK?

MY RANKING OF THE WEEK

Weekly check in

DATE _____

TOP 3 THINGS I DID THIS WEEK
- _____
- _____
- _____

MOST REWARDING INTERACTION I HAD THIS WEEK

THIS WEEK I FELT

NEXT WEEK I WANT TO
_____
_____
_____
_____

THINGS I ACCOMPLISHED THIS WEEK

WHAT WAS THE BEST THING ABOUT THE WEEK?

MY RANKING OF THE WEEK

Weekly check in

DATE _____

TOP 3 THINGS I DID THIS WEEK
- _____
- _____
- _____

MOST REWARDING INTERACTION I HAD THIS WEEK

THIS WEEK I FELT

NEXT WEEK I WANT TO
_____
_____
_____
_____

THINGS I ACCOMPLISHED THIS WEEK

WHAT WAS THE BEST THING ABOUT THE WEEK?

MY RANKING OF THE WEEK

Weekly check in

DATE _____

TOP 3 THINGS I DID THIS WEEK
- _____
- _____
- _____

THIS WEEK I FELT

NEXT WEEK I WANT TO
_____
_____
_____
_____

THINGS I ACCOMPLISHED THIS WEEK

MOST REWARDING INTERACTION I HAD THIS WEEK

WHAT WAS THE BEST THING ABOUT THE WEEK?

MY RANKING OF THE WEEK

Weekly check in

DATE _____

TOP 3 THINGS I DID THIS WEEK
- _____
- _____
- _____

MOST REWARDING INTERACTION I HAD THIS WEEK

THIS WEEK I FELT

NEXT WEEK I WANT TO
_____
_____
_____
_____

THINGS I ACCOMPLISHED THIS WEEK

WHAT WAS THE BEST THING ABOUT THE WEEK?

MY RANKING OF THE WEEK

Weekly check in

DATE _____

TOP 3 THINGS I DID THIS WEEK
- ○ _____
- ○ _____
- ○ _____

MOST REWARDING INTERACTION I HAD THIS WEEK

THIS WEEK I FELT

NEXT WEEK I WANT TO
_____
_____
_____
_____

THINGS I ACCOMPLISHED THIS WEEK

WHAT WAS THE BEST THING ABOUT THE WEEK?

MY RANKING OF THE WEEK

Weekly check in

DATE _____

TOP 3 THINGS I DID THIS WEEK
- ○ _____
- ○ _____
- ○ _____

THIS WEEK I FELT

NEXT WEEK I WANT TO
_____
_____
_____
_____

THINGS I ACCOMPLISHED THIS WEEK

MOST REWARDING INTERACTION I HAD THIS WEEK

WHAT WAS THE BEST THING ABOUT THE WEEK?

MY RANKING OF THE WEEK

www.ingramcontent.com/pod-product-compliance
Lightning Source LLC
Chambersburg PA
CBHW061134010526
44107CB00068B/2938